The Story of
MIDDLESEX
COUNTY CRICKET CLUB

Anton Rippon

Picture sources. Illustrations have been provided by: Illustrated London News Picture Library: p10, 14, 15, 16 (upper), 23, 25, 27; Marylebone Cricket Club: p10, 24, 29, 31; Mary Evans Picture Library: p12, 13 (right), 16 (lower); BBC Hulton Picture Library: p13 (left), 17, 19, 21, 39 (upper); Central Press Photos: p33-4, 36-8, 39 (lower), 40-1, 43, 45-7, 50, 53, 56, 58-9, 62, 65, 67, 74, 76, 79, 82, 88, 91-2, 94, 98, 100, 103, 104, 106-7, 109-10, 112-13, 115-16, 118-19, 122-3, 125-6, 128-9, 136 Sport and General: p49, 52, 55, 61, 64, 68, 70, 73, 77, 80, 83, 86, 89, 95, 97, 101, 133, 134; John Grainger Picture Agency: p137.

ISBN 0 86190 036 7

Printed in Great Britain by Robert Mac-Lehose & Co. Ltd., for Moorland Publishing Company Ltd., P.O. Box 2, 9-11 Station Street, Ashbourne, Derbyshire, DE6 1DZ, England.

Contents

LIST OF ILLUSTRATIONS

Early Champions

There can be few English cricket followers — even from those north of the River Trent — who do not feel some pleasure at the resurgence of Middlesex County Cricket Club over the past few years. Playing as they do at Lord's, the very headquarters of this noble game, and giving to cricket as they have, some of the greatest and most entertaining players that the game has seen, Middlesex CCC deserve success.

From the very first side led by the famous Walker brothers of Southgate, to the team which Mike Brearley has steered to success in the latter half of the 1970s and the beginning of the 1980s, Middlesex have always enjoyed the status of one of cricket's most distinguished county clubs. The names of the Hearnes, the Manns, the Studds, of Albert Trott, A. E. Stoddart, 'Patsy' Hendren, 'Plum' Warner, of Denis Compton and Bill Edrich, of John Murray and Fred Titmus have all writ themselves indelibley on cricket's role of honour. And they are but a few of the many cricketers who have made Middlesex great.

It seems that the men of Middlesex have played at cricket since first the game was invented. Certainly, in the eighteenth century, teams labelled 'Middlesex' were playing, although the pattern of the game bore little resemblence to cricket we know today. Then, it was played by the aristocracy, either between great landowners or between teams of urban and rural elevens of 'Gentlemen', and between teams of middle-class merchants and, later, between communities rather than social groups, where peers played alongside tradesmen in village and small-town teams.

From this pattern gradually emerged the county cricket we watch today, and the real starting point for the story of the present Middlesex organisation is 15 December 1863, when a meeting at the London Tavern in Bishopsgate agreed to launch Middlesex County Cricket Club. Another meeting was held on 2 February 1864 when the club officials were appointed. The first secretary, Mr C. Hillyard, noted the regular committee of sixteen members and a ground was rented from an Islington innkeeper. With the appointment was four bowlers, an umpire, a groundsman, and the later arrival of Viscount Enfield as the club's first president Middlesex CCC were ready to begin operations. The first vice-president was John Walker one of seven brothers from Southgate who were the power behind the embryo of present-day Middlesex cricket. In the summer of 1863, John Walker had assembled, at his own expense, a Middlesex eleven to meet a Kent eleven on his private ground.

The Walker brothers were all fine players and six of them played for the Gentlemen against the Players. The exception was Alfred, a fearsome underarm bowler. Today, under-arm bowling would seem almost effeminate, yet people like Alfred Walker had developed it to such a degree that he forced batsmen to move out to counter the ball's speed off the pitch. Isaac Donnithorne Walker, a fine batsman, succeeded brother Vyell Edward as skipper of Middlesex in 1873.

The Walkers were all able cricketers and administrators and they were responsible for establishing the new club. Isaac Vyell and Russell were all aggressive batsmen. In 1868, Isaac made 165 for the Gentlemen against the Players. In addition to their batting prowess, the brothers were all good bowlers. Vyell once took all ten Surrey wickets in an innings, playing for England, a feat he repeated twice more in his career with his lobs. Isaac, too, bowled lobs and Russell favoured round-arm bowling. In Middlesex's first season, when they were dismissed for 20 by MCC on 25 and 26 July 1864, still their lowest score, overarm bowling was legalised. It was the first year, also, of *Wisden Cricketer's Almanack*. John Wisden cannot have imagined that the 112-page book, selling at one shilling, (5p) would grow into the cricketer's 'bible' of today, a complete run of which would cost many thousands of **pounds.** *Wisden,* **like Middlesex, grew** into one of cricket's institutions.

About the time of Middlesex's official birth, recognisable county cricket was emerging and was about to gain the ascendency in the game. In 1846, a touring team of leading players, mostly professionals, played its first game against Twenty-two of Sheffield. **The All-England XI was founded and skippered by** Nottingham's William Clarke, one of the finest slow underarm bowlers of the day. Rebellion in the ranks had given birth to **the United England XI, formed by John** Wisden and Jem Dean in 1852. Another **split saw the United South of England XI** and eventually all these teams, which played the greater part of first-class cricket, folded, leaving the county clubs to take over.

Thomas Hearne, the most distinguished professional of the club's earliest years

Thus Middlesex County Cricket Club found itself thrust into a changing world of cricket. The new club proved to be a lusty infant, Middlesex being listed as champion county in only their third season. In 1865 they had played such teams as Sussex, Buckinghamshire and Hampshire, in addition to MCC, and wisely avoided the stronger counties such as Surrey, who were regarded as champions in Middlesex's first summer. The Surrey record of seven wins and a draw in 1864 made their status unquestionable but, by and large, there was no real format for deciding just who were the best team. In 1865, for instance, *John and James Lilleywhite's Companion* referred to Nottinghamshire thus: 'If one county were better than any other it was Nottinghamshire.' Yet all the sporting papers gave top spot to Surrey. The *Companion* gave second place to Middlesex. *Fred Lilleywhite's Guide* made Kent second, however. It was all very confusing and against this background Middlesex were named champions in 1866. The *Companion* said 'Middlesex occupy premier position,'and that would seem to be confirmed by their record of seven wins, one draw and one defeat.

In that first successful season, Middlesex beat Surrey twice by an innings and recorded two victories against Lancashire. Vyell Walker and Thomas Hearne, one of Middlesex's earliest professionals, were the side's best batsmen. Vyell Walker averaged 52 runs per innings and Hearne 35, both figures being considered exceptional batting averages at that time. In addition Hearne performed well with the ball.

These early Middlesex successes were rather tempered by the problems that they were experiencing over their ground. The landlord of the Islington venue began to use the ground for races and galas in

---

In 1787 the first match at Thomas Lord's first ground, on the site of Dorset Square, was played between Middlesex and Essex.
On 17 May 1830, the first match in which 'no balls' were recorded was played between Middlesex and MCC at Lord's.

1868 and soon after Middlesex moved to the Amateur Athletic Association Ground at Lillie Bridge, West Brompton, but that piece of land proved to be so rough that the club played at home only once during the next two years. They moved to Prince's Ground at Hans Place, Sloane Square, which was a well-known London cricket venue at that time, although it has long since been built over. Meanwhile, MCC had been tempting Middlesex to use Lord's as the club's permanent headquarters.

This was the third ground of that name. The first had been obtained by a Yorkshire man, Thomas Lord, who was an employee of the White Conduit Club, forerunner of MCC. Lord gained the lease of a piece of land situated where Dorset Square now stands and, as we have already seen, the first game to be played there was between Middlesex and Essex on 31 May and 1 June 1787. In 1811, a second Lord's was opened at North Bank, Regent's Park with turf relaid from the Dorset Square ground. Finally, a third and final move to the present Lord's was made in 1814, there apparently being few regrets among MCC members that the new Regent's Canal would cut straight through the middle of the second ground. After Lord sold out to William Ward for £5,000 in 1825, and Ward to James Dark ten years later, the ground changed hands once again in 1860 when Isaac Moses bought it, though Dark retained the lease. Finally, MCC acquired it for £18,000 in 1866 and it was to this ground that Middlesex came in 1877.

The original pavilion was destroyed by fire in 1825 and it is sad to record that the old cricket records were largely destroyed by the flames. A second pavilion was opened the following year and enlarged in 1866, together with the addition of a grandstand and a new tavern. The third pavilion, which stands today, was opened in 1890. The Mound Stand was added in 1898, and further stands followed in 1926, 1934, 1958 (the Sir Pelham Warner Stand), and 1968 (the Tavern Stand). James Lilleywhite wrote 'The addition of the Middlesex fixtures filled a decided

blank in the Marylebone programme?'

Middlesex agreed to play four county matches at Lord's in 1877. They would keep the takings and would pay all match expenses. The move turned out to be a great success and one year later Middlesex were again deemed to be champion county. They won three and drew three of their six matches but there was still no formal way of deciding the champions. The only satisfactory advancement had been the introduction, in 1873, of birth and residential qualifications for county matches. Until then players could move about and in the first Middlesex 'championship winning' season of 1866 Howitt played for both Middlesex and Nottinghamshire. After the qualification rule was introduced, a player had to decide at the start of the season whether he would play for the county of his birth or residence.

Although Middlesex were unbeaten in six games in 1878, Nottinghamshire and Yorkshire both had claims to the title. Nottinghamshire won seven, drew four and lost three games; Yorkshire won seven, drew two and lost five. Middlesex beat Yorkshire twice and drew both their games with Nottinghamshire, but what did all this prove? Although Middlesex were unbeaten, they had played only six games compared to Nottinghamshire's fourteen and Yorkshire's fourteen. *James Lilleywhite's Annual* held no clear view, and the *Companion* made two references to the fact that 'no county were champions', and another which claimed the honour for Nottinghamshire. *Wisden* today lists the 1878 Championship as 'undecided' and, with the greatest respect to Middlesex,

Middlesex circa 1878: Back row left to right: M. Flanagan, A. Burghes, Howitt (umpire), C. J. Lucas, M. Turner, R. Henderson, C. F. Buller. Front row: W. H. Hadow, A. J. Webbe, I. D. Walker, J. W. Dale, H. R. Webbe. Isaac Walker, one of the famous brothers of Southgate, scorned the use of pads against all but the fastest bowlers

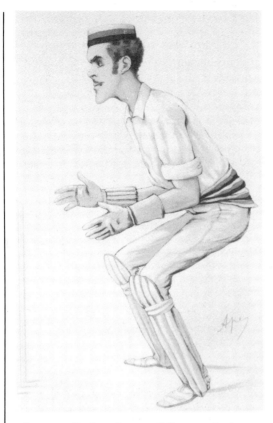

The Hon. Alfred Lyttleton, Middlesex wicketkeeper who once took off his pads in a Test Match and captured four Australian wickets. In 1883 he and Isaac Walker scored 324 for the second Middlesex wicket at Bristol

that is probably the fairest assessment.

During that season many famous names in Middlesex cricket played in the side. The Hon Edward Lyttleton averaged just over 29 and was fourth in the national batting list. He was joined around this period by such great players as C. I. Thornton and A. J. Webbe. Charles Inglis Thornton was one of cricket's hardest hitters and he is remembered for being the first cricketer to hit the ball from Scarborough into Trafalgar Square! The Trafalgar Square was, of course, the one adjacent to the Yorkshire ground, but even so, Thornton's hit carried from the **pavilion end, clean over the houses, and** into the road. It was a mighty blow and came during Thornton's hurricane 107 not out for Gentlemen of England against I. Zingari.

The Scarborough innings took Thornton only twenty-nine scoring strokes and was only one of several big-hitting sprees. At the age of eighteen he began his innings in the Eton versus Harrow match of 1868 by driving a ball clean over the old Lord's pavilion. Three years later, playing for Cambridge University against the Gentlemen of England, his first four balls went for 6, 4, 4, 6 — and this was in the days when a 6 had to be struck right out of the ground. Thornton, who also played with Kent, is credited with a hit of 168 yards and two feet at Hove, although this was in practice and some sources reckon it to be about 160 yards. Nevertheless, it was still a prodigious smite and Thornton certainly livened up Lord's when he was batting.

Middlesex's first professional, Thomas Hearne, played for the county before the formation of the present club. In all first-class matches played by a Middlesex side during 1859-75, Hearne scored 1,799 runs (average 19.77) and took 209 wickets at around 14 runs each. The county's other leading professional of the period, G. Howitt, who played during 1865-76, took 213 wickets at under 16 runs each.

Charles Thornton, known to his team-mates as 'Buns', did a tremendous amount to establish the Scarborough Cricket Festival and was given the freedom of the Yorkshire town in recognition of his services.

Alexander Josiah Webbe first played in 1875 and as player, skipper and president, his association with Middlesex lasted until 1937. He played for England just once, in 1878, and in 1887 he played two epic innings. At the start of August, Webbe made an undefeated 192 against Kent and, one week later, hammered 243 not out against Yorkshire at Huddersfield. Webbe also shared in the record first wicket stand for the Gentlemen against the Players with W. G. Grace in 1875.

After 1878, when Middlesex were claimed by some as county champions, the club's fortunes were mixed and at no time did they put in a challenge for the leadership until long after the Championship was reorganised into a format we would

A. J. Webbe. His connection with the club as player, captain and president lasted half a century

1870s and through the 1880s. The Hon Alfred Lyttleton, a fierce-hitting batsman and wicketkeeper, plundered the Gloucestershire attack in August 1883 when, together with Isaac Walker, he helped to add 324 for the second Middlesex wicket in the match at Clifton.

Dr W. G. Grace took just one wicket for 154 runs — there is no record of the doctor's comments at such humiliating treatment — and in one spell of an hour

Charles Studd, the great Middlesex and England all-rounder who retired prematurely to become a missionary in China

recognise today. Indeed, although Middlesex are listed as champions in 1866, the generally accepted year for the start of the Championship is 1873, although the adoption of the points system was not until 1887 (one point for a win, half for a draw), and the official Championship did not commence until 1890 and did not come under the jurisdiction of MCC until 1894. The earliest points scoring system of 1887-9 was fostered by the sporting press and it was only in 1890 that the county clubs themselves accepted a system of deducting defeats from victories and ignoring drawn matches. So perhaps the *proper* Championship did not start until 1895 when fourteen of today's seventeen counties competed with Worcestershire **(1899). Northamptonshire (1905) and** Glamorgan (1921) coming later. Certainly it is a matter of constant debate among cricket historians.

If Middlesex enjoyed little in the way of honours during this period of constant reorganisation as the Championship sorted itself out, then they certainly had moments of individual triumph and some of their greatest players appeared, along with Thornton and Webbe, during the late

and forty minutes, the two Middlesex batsmen scored 200 runs at a rate of two runs every minute. The Hon Alfred also enjoyed his bowling whenever he was given the chance and a year later, in the last Test at The Oval in 1884, he took four Australian wickets for 19 runs to come out of the match as England's most successful bowler. W. G. Grace took over behind the stumps to allow Lyttleton to bowl lobs, the whole England side bowling as Australia made 551.

Middlesex had a reputation for exciting and entertaining amateur batsmen and there was no more colourful character

Middlesex 1892: Back row left to right: R. S. Lucas, T. C. O'Brien, J. Phillips, J. E. West, J. T. Hearne, J. T. Rawlin. Front row: A. E. Stoddart, S. W. Scott, A. J. Webbe, E. A. Nepean, P. J. T. Henery

than Charles Studd of Cambridge University who suddenly quit cricket to become a missionary in China — and was later reported to be playing cricket in a pigtail! Besides being a fine attacking batsman, Studd was a good enough all-rounder to play for England against Australia five times. In 1882 and 1883 Studd did the double of 1,000 runs and 100 wickets in a season. Studd's brother, G. B., also played for England against the Australians and a third brother also assisted Middlesex. C. J. Ottaway of Oxford University played cricket for Middlesex and soccer for England (as did the Lyttletons, the Hon Alfred becoming a double international), and H. R. Bromley-Davenport, J. J. Sewell, G. F. Vernon and A. F. J. Ford, a fast bowler, were other amateurs who helped Middlesex at this time.

Sir Timothy O'Brien, an Irishman, kept up the tradition of hard-hitting Middlesex batsmen. Sir Timothy was particularly famous for a superb 119 against Gloucestershire and an unbeaten century in only eighty minutes off Yorkshire. He shared a fifth wicket stand of 338 for Middlesex against Sussex at Hove in June 1895 with R. S. Lucas, played for England against Australia and South Africa, becoming one of ten Oxford Blues to captain England, and, when he played for Ireland at the age of fifty-two, became one of the oldest men to have appeared in first-class cricket. Stanley Winckerworth Scott made his debut for Middlesex against Surrey in June 1878 and in the late 1880s he stood out as one of the county's most consistent batsmen. The son of an army officer, Scott was also a useful change bowler. His first Middlesex century came against Surrey in 1882 at The Oval and he topped the averages in that season and again in 1885, helped then by a splendid match against Gloucestershire at Lord's when he scored 135 not out.

Gregor MacGregor came into the Middlesex side in 1892. A Scotsman, he was a fine wicketkeeper and batsman, playing for England against Australia on both sides of the globe. MacGregor captained Middlesex, was a double Cambridge Blue at cricket and rugby, and in addition to playing cricket for England, won international caps on the rugby field for Scotland. *The Illustrated Sporting and Dramatic News* said of MacGregor: 'There have been few better wicketkeepers in the history of the game . . . in additon to operating with skill behind the stumps (he) has repeatedly made runs when other men have failed.'

Sir Timothy O'Brien, whose last first-class appearance - for Ireland - made him one of the oldest men to appear in top-class cricket. His aggressive batting was a major feature of Victorian county cricket

Throughout the 1880s, Middlesex's great amateur batsmen scored runs in a most attractive manner for the county. In 1885, the greatest of these, A. E. Stoddart played his first game for the club. Andrew Ernest Stoddart was born in South Shields in 1863 — the same year as Middlesex's birth at the London Tavern. When he was nine years old the family moved to London, fortunately for Middlesex to a house not far from Lord's, and it was inevitable that the youngster, who had played cricket in his native north-east, should find his way to the headquarters of the game. Stoddart played four games in 1885 with a highest score of 79. The following summer he made 485 in an afternoon club game for Hampstead against the Stoics (Hampstead made 813 for nine!). Stoddart was one of the most romantic figures in Eng-

lish sport during the 1880s and 1890s and he was the foremost Middlesex batsman of the time. A far abler pen than this one records his story in David Frith's superb biography *My Dear Victorious Stod*. His place in the story of Middlesex is graphically illustrated by his statistics for the club. Between 1885 and 1900 he played 167 matches, scored 9,255 runs at an average of nearly 32, with a highest score of 221 against Somerset at Lord's in his last first-class season. He scored sixteen centuries for Middlesex, twenty-eight in all first-class games, played sixteen times for England and captained his country at both cricket and rugby. A. E. Stoddart was a real-life *Boy's Own Comic* hero.

A. P. Lucas was another amateur batsman who played for both Middlesex and England around this time. A member of the Uppingham eleven of 1873, he went to Cambridge and then qualified for Surrey by residence before playing for his native Middlesex and, again through a residential qualification, for Essex. Lucas's career was not without variety then, and neither was his individual ability. Besides being a good batsman, he was a useful slow round-arm bowler and a noted outfielder. R. Slade Lucas was nother fine batsman who, according to a contemporary magazine article, 'scores at a rare pace when fairly settled down to his work.' A. P. Lucas played for England against Australia, while R. S. Lucas was a member of Lord Hawke's team which visited America. He subsequently skippered an English team which visited the West Indies.

Francis G. J. Ford was the youngest of a brotherhood of cricketers, all of whom were products of Repton School and Cambridge, and three of them played for Middlesex, F. G. J. was the most distinguished. A tall, gangling left-handed batsman who rejoiced in the nickname of 'Stork', F. G. J. hit the ball hugely to both off and left sides. A contemporary writer said of him: 'His contemptuous treatment of good fast bowling is one of the finest sights in modern cricket. He can cut, too, not with a tap but with a bang. A terribly punishing, smashing bat, yet elegant withall, and of a certain polish.' F. G. J. played five times against Australia in 1894.

These then were some of the fine amatures who steered Middlesex into what became known as the 'Golden Age' of

Gregor MacGregor, Middlesex wicketkeeper who played cricket for England and Rugby Union for Scotland

cricket. But there were professionals, too. Originally, they were players like Thomas Hearne, born in Buckinghamshire, but almost always associated with Middlesex where he played with the Walker brothers when the club was under the shadow of the cattle marked at Islington in the 1860s and G. Howitt, the bowler from Nottingham who represented the two counties in the season in which Middlesex were

declared champions for 1866. Now new professionals were making their places felt in the team, for if Middlesex could rely on amateur 'gentlemen' to score their runs, they needed the professionals to take wickets.

George Burton was the mainstay of the Middlesex attack in the 1880s and between 1881 and 1893 he took 526 wickets at 17 runs apiece — and this at a time when twelve county games a season was the most anyone played. Brown's slow-medium bowling accounted for all ten Surrey wickets at The Oval in 1888. J. E. West, another slow-medium bowler, played for Middlesex from 1885 to 1896, and in 1888 J. T. Hearne made his debut for Middlesex and started a career in which he took six for 62 against Nottinghamshire, including the wickets of the great Arthur Shrewsbury, captured the scalps of both W. G. and E. M. Grace and had match figures of eight for 91 against the Australians.

J. T. Hearne had established himself in the county team with his fast-medium bowling with which he had spun the ball sharply from the off. Hearne had a magnificent bowling action, according to his contemporaries, and he must rank among the great medium-quick bowlers in the history of cricket. His figures are phenomenal. He was one of only four bowlers to pass 3,000 wickets in a career (the others, Wilfred Rhodes, 'Tich' Freeman and Charlie Parker were all slow bowlers), in all games he did the hat-trick four times and three times in the first ten seasons he passed 200 wickets. Hearne took his one hundreth wicket of the season in 1896 as

Jim Phillips catches Arthur Shrewsbury, the great Notts batsman, at Lord's in 1892

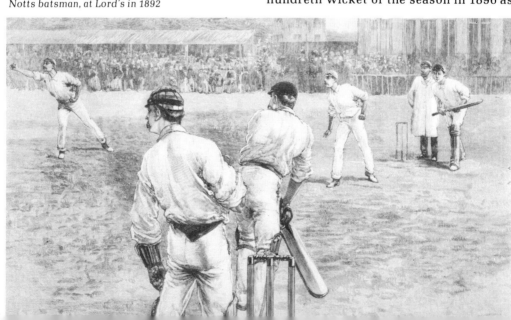

early as 12 June, and in his first-class career which lasted until 1923 he captured 3,061 at 17.75 each in all first class cricket. His haul for Middlesex alone was 2,093 a record until it was overhauled by Fred Titmus in 1973. Hearne also took forty-nine wickets in twelve Tests for England.

J. T. Hearne, like all great bowlers, needed a partner and Middlesex found one in the form of John Rawlin, rejected by his native Yorkshire but qualified for Middlesex by residence. His high delivery and brisk pace earned him ninety wickets in 1894 (104 in all first-class games) and his batting was also of great service to Middlesex on occasions. In that same season Rawlin shared in a stand of 150 with R. S. Lucas at The Oval. Jim Phillips, a slow round-arm bowler, alternated between England and Australia, playing for Middlesex in our summer before going off to appear with the Melbourne Club.

> **J. T. Hearne effectively ended his first class career in 1914 at the age of forty-seven. But in 1923 he played in one more first-class match, against Scotland, to become one of the oldest men to appear in first-class cricket.**

During this period Middlesex enjoyed some exciting matches and none more so than in 1886 when they almost defeated the Australians. The tourists needed 123 to win the match and Middlesex had them at 120 for nine. Middlesex failed to capture the final wicket and the Australians got home. But it had been a nail-biting finish, thanks to some excellent bowling from Burton (six for 56) and West (three for 25). Earlier, Middlesex wicketkeeper, G. Spillman, had scored a valuable 87 and J. G. Walker (the Oxford Blue, not to be confused with John Walker, who went to Cambridge and who died on 14 August 1885) and made 67.

In 1888 Middlesex beat Nottinghamshire for the first time in twenty-two years, by an innings and 55 runs. In 1889 O'Brien led the charge as Middlesex made 280 to beat Yorkshire in well under three hours at Lord's. O'Brien's contribution being the eighty-minute century referred to earlier. In 1894 Middlesex followed on 179 behind against Surrey but, thanks to O'Brien and Stoddart, who made 228

J. T. Hearne, one of cricket's greatest bowlers who set a Middlesex record which would last for decades

before the first wicket fell, and bowling of the highest calibre from Hearne and Rawlin, managed to win after rattling out their neighbours for 119. In this period Middlesex had managed to attain third place in 1891, the season in which Stoddart scored an unbeaten 215 against Lancashire. In carrying his bat through the Middlesex innings at Old Trafford, Stoddart made the highest score of the season in five hours. Hearne and Rawlin then got to work and Middlesex triumphed by an innings.

The Golden Age

The start of cricket's 'Golden Age' saw Middlesex finish joint sixth with Warwickshire. The 1895 season was notable for the stand of 338 between O'Brien and R. S. Lucas at Brighton when O'Brien became the third Middlesex batsman to score a double century for the county with 202 off the Sussex attack. J. T. Hearne topped one hundred wickets in only eighteen Championship matches. In 1896 Middlesex finished in third spot. James Douglas, who was one of Middlesex's most reliable opening batsmen for several years, had a fine season, averaging 30 and in one fortnight in August, sharing, with Stoddart, in opening stands of 178 against Yorkshire at Bradford, 158 against Nottinghamshire at Trent Bridge, and 166 against Kent at Lord's.

During the season Rawlin had the misfortune to make a duck during his benefit match with Somerset at Lord's, although Middlesex won by an innings with J. T. Hearne taking twelve wickets while poor Rawlin could manage none. Rawlin had better luck against Surrey at The Oval where he took eight wickets in the match which Middlesex won by 205 runs. Hearne again took twelve wickets and O'Brien scored a masterly 137 on a rain-affected pitch. It was a different story when the teams met at Lord's. Here, Middlesex lost after batting second on a crumbling pitch and being bowled out for 83 in their second innings. Tom Richardson took ten Middlesex wickets in the match.

Middlesex had been third in the table in four of the previous six seasons but in 1897 they slipped back to seventh where they were coincidently coupled with Warwickshire again. Stoddart played only nine games due to injury and, with O'Brien unable to reproduce his usual form it was as well that Francis Ford was available more often and his 150 against Gloucestershire was just one of many valuable innings he played that summer. The forty-year-old Rawlin was now struggling to maintain his bowling form and Hearne was very much on his own until C. M. Wells, formerly of Surrey, became available in the school holidays. Wells was a teacher and could only play in the second part of each season. Rawlin, meanwhile, was used more as a batsman in the autumn of his career and he made his first century at the age of forty-two.

In 1898 Middlesex were back up to second place. There were two memorable games against the eventual champions, Yorkshire, when Middlesex lost by an innings at Lord's, despite Ford's brave 127 out of a total of 170, but won at Headingley. They dismissed Yorkshire for 45 runs in their second innings and then scored 62 for two to win by eight wickets. The damage was done by Albert Trott, who took seven for 13 as the Yorkshiremen slumped on the second day. Trott was an Australian, from Victoria, who bowled leg-breaks out of a huge hand. Coupled with a fast yorker, and a few more inventive balls, Trott's bowling earned him 200 wickets in each of the following two seasons. His batting, too, was good enough to earn him the distinction of becoming the first man to pass 1,000 runs and 200 wickets in one season, and he is remembered as the only man ever to clear the present Lord's pavilion — a feat he was forever trying to repeat, to the detriment of his batting.

One batsman who did especially well in 1898 was Pelham Francis Warner who averaged over 33 runs per innings. 'Plum' Warner, as he became known, was an Oxford Blue, educated at Rugby, and went on to become probably the greatest single influence the establishment of Middlesex as a major force in the game. He was an entertaining batsman with a good, upright stance and became one of the county's most consistent batsmen as well as a great servant of England. He hit sixty centuries in first-class cricket and in 1937 he was knighted for his services to the game, becoming President of MCC in 1950. Warner had played for Middlesex since 1894, making his debut against Somerset at Taunton in August and scoring 6 and 4 when Middlesex won by 19 runs. This great Middlesex and England batsman was actually born in Trinidad where his father was Attorney-General of the island.

In 1899 Middlesex were again second with Surrey as champions. This was the first of Albert Trott's two epic seasons. As well as taking 200 wickets he played some great innings. His best was 164 against Yorkshire, a performance which began sedately and then wound up into a hurricane finish. At the same match 'Plum' Warner scored 150, which was his first century for Middlesex. In the same season Trott made his mighty hit over the Lord's pavilion. On 31 July he cleared the roof when batting for MCC against the Australians, the unlucky bowler being M. A. Noble. Playing for MCC aginst Sussex a few weeks earlier, Trott actually struck a bigger blow, but that shot, thumped off the bowling of Fred Tate, hit the MCC coat-of-arms sited above the roof and fell back into the seats.

1899 was the year in which Rawlins made his sole century, helping Middlesex to beat Surrey at Lord's. At The Oval, Francis Ford made 147 to save the game for Middlesex, while C. M. Wells scored 244 off the Nottinghamshire attack and then weighed in with match figures of nine for 111. Stoddart had played his last full season in 1898 when he led the side in Webbe's absence and headed the batting averages with 52.95 and 1,000 runs for the third time in his career. Sadly, the great cricketer then bowed out of first-class cricket, declining the Middlesex captaincy which instead passed from Webbe to MacGregor. Stoddart played just once in 1899. Sussex allowed him to take the place of Dr George Thornton who withdrew after fielding on the first day. Middlesex made 466 but Stoddart was bowled for a duck. The visit of the Australians to Lord's for the county match saw Middlesex hammered by an innings and 230 runs.

In 1900 Middlesex went back down to share seventh place with Surrey and Gloucestershire. Middlesex's season was in two halves of contrasting fortune. In their first nine games they won only once;

Albert Trott, Australian all-rounder who became the first man to pass 1,000 runs and take 200 wickets in a season. In 1899 he became the only man to clear the Lord's pavilion

in their last thirteen they triumphed eight times. Surrey were beaten twice in a season for the first time since 1893 with Hearne capturing sixteen of their wickets in the two games and taking ninety-five in all. Albert Trott started slowly but from the end of June he swept county batsmen away with disdain and took 211 wickets in all games to complete a rare double for the second season in succession.

The Surrey games were full of incidents. At The Oval, Hearne and a number ten batsman, W. Williams, edged Middlesex to victory by scoring 18 runs with nine wickets down; at Lord's, Hearne and Trott rattled out Surrey for 64 in their second innings after Warner had scored one of his five centuries that season. Warner finished 1900 with 1,335 runs and an average of close on 45. Bernard James Tindal Bosanquet, immortal as the inventor of the googly, made a century in each innings against Leicestershire, scoring 136 and 139 at Lord's in July 1900. Bosanquet began his first-class career with Oxford University and this performance against Leicestershire confirmed him as one of the most exciting batsmen of the era. The real highlight of the Middlesex summer was, however, the last innings for the county by A. E. Stoddart. Stoddart had played against Sussex in May when he was bowled for just a single. He re-appeared for J. T. Hearne's benefit match against

A. E. Stoddart, a magnificent batsman who retired at the height of his powers

Somerset over Whitsun and was out for 12 in the first innings, hitting out at the last ball before lunch.

When Middlesex batted again they were 69 runs behind when Stoddart and his Hampstead colleague, H. B. Hayman, started to knock off the deficit. How they succeeded! The pair added 151 before Hayman was out and, after young George Beldam had stayed for a while, R. W. Nicholls helped Stoddart to put on a further 152. Stoddart went on mercilessly. He cut and drove his way to 221 before advancing down the wicket to Lewis and being stumped, yards out of his crease. With that epic innings completed, Stoddart walked back to the Lord's pavilion and out of Middlesex cricket. As his figure disappeared through the dressing room door, so too did a career which promised so much more. It was a tragic loss to the game.

1900 was the era of the great men Gilbert Jessop and K. S. Ranjitsinhji. Jessop scored 109 in only sixty-seven minutes off the Middlesex attack at Lord's in June; in August, Ranji hammered the attack for 202 at Hove, adding 88 runs in just over half an hour with the legendary C. Aubrey Smith who later became a film star and started the famous Hollywood cricket colony. This was indeed cricket's 'Golden Age'.

These were also yo-yo years for Middlesex. In 1901 they were back to second place behind Yorkshire, who were in the middle of their hat-trick of Championships. Middlesex's batting was again the club's mainstay and ten batsmen reached centuries with Warner enjoying three such innings. Warner scored 1,382 runs in the Championship at 49, and Bosanquet, with two centuries, also topped the 1,000-mark. James Douglas, also a scorer of two centuries, notched over 700 runs. H. B. Chinnery also managed a century, though he only played seven innings for Middlesex in his career, and Albert Trott enjoyed 112 against Essex in the last game of the season.

The bowling was less impressive. Hearne had a poor season and it was Trott (eighty-nine wickets at 23.57) who topped the averages. Bosanquet and Wells each had barely adequate returns and Rawlin, the 'daddy' of the attack, took five for 88 against Surrey who made 559 for eight at

The Oval. But this performance apart, Rawlin had a poor season, too. This, incidently, was the second season in which the over was increased from five balls to six, and the optional follow-on introduced. Ten matches were drawn, a measure of Middlesex's lack of bowling penetration.

If the start of a new century had given Middlesex hope, then the 1902 season was a disaster. In a wet summer the side won only three Championship games and went from second to twelfth in the table, losing twice to Surrey. This time the batting as well as the bowling let them down. Only James Douglas impressed. The only bowling highlights were at Lord's when Hearne did the hat trick against Essex. Rain prevented play on the first two days and although the match was an inevitable draw, those spectators who did turn up were rewarded with twenty-four wickets on the last day. At Trent Bridge, Gregor MacGregor stumped five Nottinghamshire batsmen in the home side's second innings, four of them off the bowling of Bosanquet.

The 1903 season was similar to 1902 regarding the depressing weather. But for Middlesex it seemed as though the sun shone every day for they surprised everyone, including perhaps themselves, by taking the County Championship for the first time since it had been reorganised. Middlesex went undefeated until the second week of August when Yorkshire beat them by 230 runs after the champions of the previous summer skittled Middlesex out for 79 in the first innings, Hirst and Rhodes inflicting the damage. The rain prevented another clear-cut result until the last game at The Oval. George Beldam scored his second century of the summer against Surrey and then Trott and Hearne bowled them out for 57. When they followed on, it was Wells who led the slaughter with five wickets as Middlesex won by an innings. It was a victory which added to seven other Middlesex wins to give them the title.

Beldam had a fine season, scoring 854 runs and heading the averages. Bosanquet and Warner both recaptured their lost form of the previous season and the Cambridge Blue, L. J. Moon, scored two centuries. Moon played only a few games each year — he had not appeared at all in

B. J. T. Bosanquet, inventor of the 'googly'

1902 — but he could always be relied upon for useful runs. Although Douglas made his highest score that season, 204 off Gloucestershire, he failed in almost every other game. The Middlesex bowling was back to its best and there was all-round rejoicing at Lord's. The match against The Rest at The Oval saw the Champion County enjoy the best of the spoils.

In 1904 Middlesex could not repeat the Championship success but they still did well in finishing fourth. Bosanquet had a fine season with the ball, taking over fifty wickets, and there were exciting wins over Surrey by two wickets (where Albert Trott played an uncharacteristic innings to help MacGregor pull Middlesex through), and by one wicket against Kent. It was also Bosanquet's season with the bat and he passed 1,000 runs. George Beldam had the delight of adding 201 for the fifth wicket against Somerset at Lord's in partnership with his brother E. A. Beldam. Both men scored centuries in a stand which took under two hours. Hearne took fifteen wickets in the match.

Warner and Douglas both had good seasons and there was an exciting tied game with the South African tourists, Bosanquet scoring 110 and 44. There were failures — Trott failed to reach double figures nine times in a row and R. W. Nicholls began with four ducks, ended with a 'pair' and failed to average 6 runs an innings.

But of all the performances in 1904 perhaps that of R. E. More was most spectacular. More had an undistinguished Middlesex career, yet against Yorkshire at Sheffield, batting number ten, he scored an electrifying 120 not out in only 100 minutes. He added 128 in forty-eight minutes with Bosanquet (who made 141), and 91 with Hearne in fifty-two minutes.

Middlesex slipped to eleventh place in 1905, due to some all-round failures. Only Bosnaquet, Warner and Douglas batted well throughout, Bosanquet making three centuries, but overall there was no consistency. Trott failed with both bat and ball, Beldam played little and with scant success, and three amateurs who promised much on their fleeting appearances — E. Field, C. C. Page and J. H. Stogden — were never in the side long enough to make a difference. Only Hearne returned reasonable bowling figures and *Wisden* commented that the Middlesex fielding was at a particularly low ebb.

The season saw the first appearance of Frank Tarrant. Tarrant, like Trott and Roche, was a Victorian. This first season was unremarkable, save for one innings of 162 not out at Leyton when he shared in an unfinished ninth wicket stand of 98 with Hearne who made 56, his highest score (Hearne had also taken eight for 93). Soon, however, the Australian would do the double with regularity and become one of the greatest all-rounders of the day. His left-arm spin and concientious batting made him a tremendous asset to Middlesex for whom he scored more than 12,000 runs and took more than 1,000 wickets.

Another arrival in 1905 was E. Mignon. He, too, had a fairly inauspicious start but went on to take over 400 wickets in nine seasons of fast bowling. Middlesex's importation of Tarrant, however, caused some ill-feeling, as did the arrival of Trott and Roche in the latter years of the 1890s. The 1906 *Wisden* commented: 'We need not in this place, whatever we may think, go into the question of whether Middlesex ought to import bowlers from the Colonies instead of striving to discover native-born talent.' And speaking of Trott's indifferent season, *Wisden* made the observation: 'if Trott were a man of forty or more, we should despair of him . . .' In all, Middlesex won only four games, losing seven as well as going down to the Australians by 132 runs at Lord's. Armstrong took eight for 50 in Middlesex's second innings.

Middlesex were again eleventh in 1906, winning only four matches, two of them against Lancashire. Tarrant established himself in the side with seventy-three wickets as well as being one of only three players to score a century for Middlesex. Warner scored two and the other was notched by Bosanquet who played in only three matches. Mignon also prospered

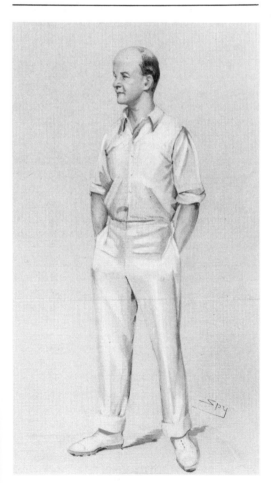

'Plum' Warner, probably the greatest single influence on the establishment of Middlesex as a major force in cricket

The 1903 County Champions: Back row left to right: J. T. Hearne, R. W. Nicholls, B. J. T. Bosanquet, J. T. Rawlin. Middle row: L. J. Moon, C. M. Wells, G. MacGregor, P. F. Warner, G. W. Beldam. Front row: J. Douglas, A. E. Trott, E. A. Beldam. Douglas scored 204 at Bristol during the season but failed in almost every other game

with the ball, taking sixty-eight wickets at just over 25 runs each, but the great J. T. Hearne achieved little and with thirty-four wickets at nearly 31 runs each, he had lost much of his best form. Another player who found lean times was Albert Trott, although he did manage to take five wickets against Lancashire at Lord's. With Warner now the only amateur to be available on a regular basis, Middlesex rung the team changes, but with little success in finding a winning combination.

Middlesex entered the 1907 season with a more settled side and for them it was a period when until the cessation of cricket for World War 1, they were never out of the top six in the Championship. There were several success stories in this period. Albert Trott enjoyed a revival and in his benefit match against Somerset at Lord's he took a double hat-trick in the same innings. Somerset needed 264 to win when Trott took four wickets in four balls and then followed up that feat with another three in succession to give him

seven for 20 and Middlesex victory by 166 runs. Trott is one of the only seven players to take two hat-tricks in the same match and only one of them — J. S. Rao, playing for Services against Northern Punjab at Amristar in 1963-4, managed it in the same innings also.

In 1907, Frank Tarrant also took four wickets in four balls at Bristol and the Australian all-rounder had a fine season. He did the double, scoring 147 against Somerset at Taunton one week before his hat-trick. Tarrant's 1,552 runs and 183 wickets this season underlined just what a great all-rounder he was. Trott had ninety-six wickets and J. T. Hearne had some fine returns — a match analysis of eleven for 67 at Old Trafford and ten for 71 at Trent Bridge. The batting, too, was solid. Warner scored a century before lunch at The Oval and finished the season with 1,353 runs at nearly 45 per innings. His opening stand with James Douglas (79) realised 232 in 150 minutes.

The other surprises were a fine win over

Sussex when Tarrant took eight for 49 to bowl out the opposition for 84 when they needed only 96 to win; and a game at Sheffield where George Hirst took nine for 45 when Middlesex were dismissed for 91. There was also sensation in the match with Lancashire at Lord's when the Lancashire captain refused to continue

Australian Frank Tarrant, one of cricket's finest all-round players. Between 1904 and 1914 he scored over 12,000 runs and took 1,000 wickets for Middlesex

the game, alleging that the public had ruined it by walking across the square. Archie MacLaren's side were 57 for one after the first day and had been restricted to just twenty-five overs due to rain. A crowd of about 500 paid for the second day but no play was possible and some of them wandered across the pitch to voice their annoyance in front of the Lord's pavilion. Without consulting the Middlesex skipper, MacLaren called off the game, saying that the pitch had been 'deliberately torn up' by the public. The third day of the match dawned fine and

the pitch looked in good shape — but the Lancashire side had gone home. Middlesex might have been able to claim the match by default, but they did not and it is listed as a draw.

In 1908, the Middlesex batting had a golden year. If the bowling had been as strong then Middlesex would surely have improved on their eventual fourth position. With the demise of MacGregor, Warner became official Middlesex captain, having lead the side often in MacGregor's absence Warner did not let the burdens of captaincy affect his individual play. He scored five centuries that summer, the same number as Tarrant who did exceptionally well with the ball again, returning the best figures of any Middlesex bowler. Bosanquet was available for nine games and scored two centuries, averaging over 50. It was a sad fact that this would be his last season as a Middlesex regular.

L. J. Moon and C. C. Page were available regularly and both contributed well with the bat and MacGregor's place behind the stumps was taken by the amateurs Page and Bird, and by the former Kent professional H. R. Murrell, who was already in the side as a solid batsman and had deputised when MacGregor was absent in previous seasons. Murrell had to wait until 1909 to make the position his own, playing with distinction for several seasons. Warner shared in four opening stands of over 150, three with Moon and one with Tarrant. Warner and Moon added 203 before being parted in the opening game of the season against Hampshire when Middlesex made 502 for nine. The others were 212 against Sussex, 161 against Nottinghamshire, and 158 against Hampshire, this time at Bournemouth. It was certainly a season of big scores and there were two more Middlesex totals which passes 500 — 596 against Somerset and 534 for eight declared against Nottinghamshire.

> Frank Tarrant, who played for Middlesex from 1905 to 1914, scored 12,169 runs for the county, average 38.03, and took 1,005 wickets at 17.43 each. In all first-class games in England, Tarrant scored nearly 16,000 runs and took 1,335 wickets.

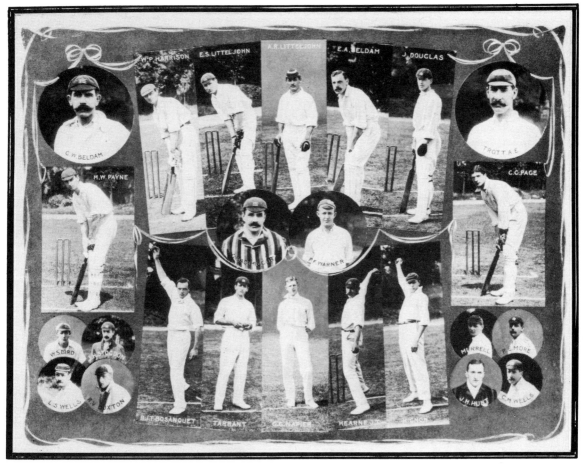

Middlesex players of 1907

Batting helmets are considered a recent innovation, but when batting against the West Indies at Lord's in 1933 'Patsy' Hendren created a mild sensation when he appeared in a special cap. It was made by his wife and had three peaks, two of them covering his ears and temples. The cap was lined with sponge rubber and Hendren said that he needed protection against 'the new-fashioned persistant short-pitched bouncers.'

'Young Jack' Hearne was only 20 when he scored 114 for England against Australia at Melbourne during the 1911-12 MCC tour. Against Essex at Leyton in 1914, he scored an unbeaten 106 and took fourteen for 146.

But these big scores were not matched by the bowling. After Tarrant, Mignon was the next most successful with fifty wickets, while Albert Trott enjoyed no sensations like those of 1907. In fact, the man who had two golden seasons around the turn of the century was soon to bow out. But two players who were at Lord's and would become major contributors to the story of Middlesex were the Hon C. N. Bruce, who would come into his own after the war, and one Elias Hendren, better known the world over as 'Patsy' after his Irish ancestry. After an inauspicious start at Lord's, Hendren went on to become one of the greatest batsmen the game has ever seen. A short, stocky man he drove and cut with immense power and was never afraid to hook the fastest bowlers.

Middlesex were sixth in 1909 when Hendren played regularly and another great name in Middlesex cricket, J. W. Hearne, played his first game. J. W. and J. T. Hearne were cousins and a third, T. J.

Hearne, is credited with one appearance, though as he 'played' in a one-day defeat of the touring Philadelphians and arrived too late to field and was not needed to bat, he can hardly be said to have had a career with the club! J. W. Hearne was a different proposition. He started slowly and was actually dropped for a spell. But after returning for the final match of 1909 and scoring 71 against Somerset, he went on to become one of England's greatest all-rounders. A stylish batsman and wonderful leg-break and googly bowler. J. W. Hearne went on to score 37,252 runs in all first-class cricket, including ninety-six centuries, at an average of 40.98, took 1,839 wickets at 24.42 each and held 329 catches. He retired in 1936.

Another new face this season was Frank Mann, the Cambridge cricket and rugby Blue. F. T. Mann was a stylish and powerful batsman who served Middlesex well for many seasons. Mann and Hearne played their first seasons for Middlesex in a wet summer. Only Tarrant reached 1,000 runs for Middlesex and in the game at Bristol, the Australian practically beat Gloucestershire single-handed in one day. He carried his bat when making 55 out of Middlesex's 145 and helped bowl out the home side for 33 and 81, taking thirteen wickets in the match, including a hat-trick in the second innings. Tarrant took 108 wickets to head both batting and bowling averages. His wickets cost just over 17 runs each while his nearest rival was J. T. Hearne with fifty-one at 25 runs each.

'Patsy' Hendren scored nearly 700 runs at an average of nearly 20 and a top score of 75. 'Plum' Warner scored three centuries for the county and Tarrant hit two, these players being the only Middlesex centurions of the season. They were, of course, the two leading Middlesex batsmen while the Cambridge batsman, W. P. Robertson,

was their nearest rival in the county averages with around 21 runs per innings. Thanks largely to the weather, Middlesex drew nearly half their Championship matches and suffered financially from the loss of so much cricket at Lord's.

The 1910 season saw Middlesex finish third with J. T. Hearne coming back to full form with 116 wickets for Middlesex alone to head the national bowling averages. Albert Trott, on the other hand, played only three games and then was not seen again in Middlesex colours. He had not long to live and shot himself in 1914. Tarrant was again outstanding with both bat and ball and J. W. Hearne, scored his first Middlesex century (155 against Somerset at Lord's) and taking nearly fifty wickets in the season including a marvellous spell at Lord's of seven wickets in five overs for two runs against Essex. Hendren and Mann were on top of their game and Hendren's best performance came when he was the only batsman, apart from Warner, to come to terms with the Gloucestershire attack on a difficult pitch. He made 91 and then saw Tarrant and J. T. Hearne bowl Middlesex to an innings victory.

The 1910 season was notable for a surprise win over Yorkshire. Middlesex had been dismissed for 72 and the Yorkshiremen stood almost 100 runs on with seven wickets in hand when J. T. and J. W. Hearne set about them and soon they were all out with a lead restricted to 118. Warner and Tarrant put 137 for the first wicket and then J. T. Hearne took six for 20 as Middlesex won by 123 runs. There were defeats, of course. Kent scored 500 for eight and then bowled out Middlesex for 105 and 197; Surrey rattled them out for 41 at The Oval; and Yorkshire had revenge at Lord's, scoring 331 to win with two wickets and one ball to spare.

Middlesex were third again in 1911. Tarrant headed the batting averages with over 50 and A. R. Littlejohn headed the bowling averages with forty-six wickets at 16.95. J. W. Hearne continued to establish himself as one of England's leading all-rounders. He scored 1,427 runs at 44.59 for Middlesex and took eighty-seven wickets, a performance which earned him a trip to Australia with MCC that winter. Tarrant also took eighty-seven wickets while J. T. Hearne captured

> **Albert Trott, who burst upon the Test Match scene in 1894-5 with eight for 43 for Australia against England, and had a batting average of over 100 for the series, came to Middlesex after being largely ignored by the selectors in later seasons. He met a tragic end on the eve of World War I when he shot himself at his London lodgings.**

Middlesex enjoy the idyllic setting of Cambridge University in 1912. The Hon. H. G. J. Mullholland on his way to 74 off the Middlesex attack

108. J. W. Hearne did the hat-trick against Essex and Tarrant also achieved the feat against Somerset. J. W. Hearne also scored an undefeated 234 against Somerset at Lord's. Warner and Tarrant scored four centuries each, E. S. Littlejohn three, and Hendren also scored his first century for Middlesex.

The Littlejohn brothers had enjoyed a field day against Lancashire at Lord's with E. S. hitting 105 — his three centuries for Middlesex in 1911 came in only eight games — while A. R. captured fifteen wickets for 189 runs. In 1912, E. S. Littlejohn head the batting averages with 43.30 from his 389 runs as Middlesex slipped a little to fifth place. Warner, who was taken ill on his second Australian tour, was missing for much of the season and with J. W. Hearne also finding an Australian tour something of a strain, Middlesex did not have the same power as the previous summer. It was a damp summer and batting was always difficult. Only four centuries were scored for Middlesex, one by E. S. Littlejohn and one by Tarrant, while Warner, despite that he played only in eight games, scored the other two.

Only Tarrant of the regular batsmen, averaged just over 30, a measure of the damp summer, and only Hendren, who had a top score of 97, came near him. The bowlers faired differently, of course, and Tarrant, J. W. Hearne, and J. T. Hearne — who did the hat-trick against Warwickshire — all returned good averages. The highlight of a summer which saw little

sun was the defeat of Yorkshire. Middlesex were the only side to beat the 1912 champions. Yorkshire were bowled out for 157 and Middlesex then took a lead of 28. Tarrant took six Yorkshire second innings wickets to leave Middlesex 139 to win. They got them with six wickets down.

In 1913, J. W. Hearne, 'Young Jack' as he was known, finished his Middlesex season with 1,663 runs at an average of over 51 runs per innings. Hearne scored four centuries as he led the county's batsmen in a season when they finished sixth. Warner, Tarrant and Hendren followed Hearne, and Hendren's aggregate for Middlesex alone topped 1,000 runs for the first time. True, the summer favoured batsmen much more than the soggy 1912 season, although when two Championship games were started on a Saturday as an experiment — one at The Oval, the other against Hampshire at Lord's — rain washed out the first day's play for Middlesex. Around this time Championship games started on Mondays and Thursdays and often the last day on a Saturday came to an early close, thus robbing clubs of what should have been their best pay day through the gates.

In 1913 Harry Murrell (who was always known as 'Joe' to his teammates) shared in a record eight-wicket stand with M. H. C. Doll. The pair added an unbroken 182 against Nottinghamshire.

Frank Mann hit his first century for Middlesex when he rescued them at 39 for five and scored a rapid 135. When he was last out, 199 had been added and the Worcestershire bowlers had a few muttered curses as Mann was applauded into the Lord's pavilion. Tarrant was also in fine form this season. When Middlesex were beaten by an innings at Liverpool — being bowled out for 125 and 159, Tarrant alone stood firm with 58 in the first innings and 81 not out in the second. Tarrant then took thirteen wickets as Middlesex beat Surrey at Lord's. They might have won at The Oval, too, had it not been for Jack Hobbs. Surrey followed on 211 behind but Hobbs, with an undefeated 144, thwarted Middlesex. Champions Kent beat Middlesex twice — by five runs and by seven wickets in a low scoring game at Maidstone, but in the next game Middlesex totalled 548 for eight declared (J.W.Hearne 189). Although Tarrant had eleven wickets in the match, a last-wicket Hampshire stand of 91 denied Middlesex victory.

The 1914 season was marked by the performances of Frank Tarrant and J. W. Hearne. They shared in several big stands together as Middlesex finished runners-up to Surrey, and might well have taken the Championship had not war intervened Middlesex had lost only once — an innings defeat on a tricky Maidstone pitch — when they met Yorkshire at Sheffield. The outbreak of war on 4 August 1914 meant that Middlesex went into the match without Warner and other key players. Yorkshire won by two wickets and Surrey went to the top of the table. When the leaders' last two games were cancelled due to The Oval being requisitioned for the war effort, Surrey were declared champions. Middlesex had revenge over Kent in their last game when Frank Tarrant and J. T. Hearne, playing in their last game for Middlesex, bowled their side to a 298-run victory.

But it was Tarrant and the other Hearne — J. W. — who stole the thunder of 1914. The two put on a record 380 for the second wicket against Lancashire at Lord's and headed the Middlesex batting averages by a mile. Hearne had 2,021 runs, averaging nearly 75, and Tarrant, 1,743 at an average of over 51. In the win over Kent, J. W. scored 118 not out and took valuable second innings wickets; and against Surrey at The Oval, after Middlesex had been hit all round the ground for over 500 runs, J. W. rescued the side with a wondrous undefeated 191 in their second innings. The two players also excelled with the ball. Tarrant headed the averages with 131 wickets at 18.40 each and J. W. came second with 114 at 21.42. Tarrant had a splendid match at Old Trafford, scoring 101 not out and taking sixteen wickets for 176; and Hearne took ten wickets in the match against Essex at Lord's and scored 88 and 37 not out.

But if it was Tarrant, J. W. Hearne, and, to a lesser extend, J. T. Hearne, who could look back on the 1914 season with exceptional pride, then the other Middlesex players who contributed so much to this fine side must not be forgotton. Hendren, W. P. Robertson, the Cambridge Blue, and Harry Lee, who joined the side a couple of years earlier, made the batting even stronger and Lee enjoyed his first century scoring 139 against Nottinghamshire. Nineteen centuries were scored for Middlesex, seven by J. W. Hearne and five by Tarrant, while there were many other batsmen, including some 'occasional' amateurs who gave solid support. Though overshadowed by his cousin, J. T. Hearne still returned fine bowling figures in his last season, and behind the stumps, Harry Murrell continued to perform superbly. Although the Kaiser denied them the Championship (with a little help from the MCC perhaps, who decided that Surrey could have the title in less than satisfactory circumstances), this Middlesex eleven was one of the club's strongest-ever. Even the ravages of war would not deny them their due when peace was restored.

Champions Again – And Challengers

English cricket, like so many other institutions, struggled to come to terms with post-war life and the 1919 season was an unsatisfactory one with the experiment of three two-day games per week largely failing, due to the strenuous nature of the programme. Middlesex were without J. T. Hearne and Tarrant, and several players who had died in the war, including L. J. Moon who, although he had played only a few matches for Middlesex each season, had contributed valuable runs. Now Middlesex faced the new world scene with some new faces. They finished thirteenth in the Championship and a measure of their weak attack was that J. W. Hearne, despite suffering from a finger injury, still finished with more wickets (forty-three) than any other bowler. Dr C. H. Gunasekara, a fine all-rounder from Ceylon, took thirty-six. Dr Churchill Hector Gunasekara was denied a Cambridge Blue only by the outbreak of the war. He was a fine all-round sportsman who won his colours at Royal College, Colombo, for soccer and athletics, played cricket twelve times for Ceylon, captaining them on nine occasions, and was the Ceylon lawn tennis singles champion and partner in the double championship. Nigel Haig took thirty wickets and Greville Stevens twenty-four.

Stevens was the most significant find of 1919. He was a fine batsman and leg-

The 1920 Champions: Back row left to right: H. W. Lee H. K. Longman, F. J. Durston, N. Haig, G. T. S. Stevens, C. H. L. Skeet. Front row: J. W. Hearne, F. T. Mann, P. F. Warner, H. R. Murrell, E. H. Hendren

break and googly bowler and that season he became the first schoolboy to represent the Gentlemen against the Players at Lord's, after scoring 466 in a house match at University College School. On his first-class debut for Middlesex, against Hampshire at Lord's, he took ten wickets for 136, and if business committments had not interrupted his career, he would have improved greatly on a still excellent career record of 10,361 runs at 29.69, and 676 wickets at 26.55 in all first-class cricket. In addition he was a fine close fielder who held over 200 catches. Stevens gained his Oxford Blue as a Freshman and played in ten Tests for England.

The batting was headed by Hendren who hit 1,258 runs for Middlesex, while Warner scored just one century, against Australian Imperial Forces team. Warner was by now forty-five and he found the hours of play during this year of two-day Championship games were too much for his frail health. The games were staged from 11.30am to 7.30pm on the first day and from 11.00am to 7.30pm on the second. Warner thought seriously about giving up the captaincy there and then, but A. J. Webbe persuaded him to continue. Bosanquet and Robertson both played in this first post-war season and did well with the bat, although Frank Mann enjoyed only moderate success. Highlights of the season included a score of 608 for seven against Hampshire when two Middlesex batsmen, Hearne and Hendren, scored double centuries at Lord's. Hearne made 218 not out and Hendren 201 in a stand between the two of 325, a record for Middlesex's fourth wicket. This was the match in which Stevens took ten wickets on his first-class debut for Middlesex as they won by an innings and 74 runs.

The Hon C. N. Bruce reappeared for Middlesex and in the match with Lancashire at Lord's he scored 149 at more than a run a minute in the first innings and 51 in just over half an hour in the second when Middlesex attacked a target they finally failed to reach. Surrey beat Middlesex by an innings at The Oval and drew at Lord's; and the 1919 champions, Yorkshire, won at Headingley and drew at Lord's. Kent might have taken the title but, in the last game of the season, they failed to repeat their earlier innings win over Middlesex at Maidstone. The Championship went to

Yorkshire, but Middlesex would soon wrest it from their grasp.

On the last day of July 1920 Middlesex were lying sixth in the Championship with no apparent hope of taking the title. On the last day of August they completed an improbable defeat of Surrey at Lord's — their ninth successive win — to become county champions for the first time since 1903. The Championship was decided on a percentage basis of points gained per match, with not every side playing the same number of games. Five points were awarded for a win, and three points for the lead in a drawn game. When no first innings lead had been decided, the game did not count and no points were awarded. Middlesex started well with innings defeats over Warwickshire and Sussex, followed by a draw against Lancashire and defeat at the hands of Nottinghamshire. Four of the next five games were won. Then Essex clipped their wings. Middlesex took first innings points in the game at Lord's and lost by just 4 runs at Leyton. Amazingly, in the second match, Warner was well set with 22 not out when he had to retire to return to Lord's and help select the Test side.

Thus, Middlesex, after their bright start did not look likely champions. But Stevens took thirteen wickets for 60 runs to beat Sussex by an innings, and Hearne took eight for 26 to earn them a nail-biting 5-run win at Canterbury. Surrey and Nottinghamshire were both beaten easily before Yorkshire went within a hair's breadth of winning at Bradford when Middlesex got their last man out with four runs to spare. Somerset, Warwickshire and Kent again fell as Middlesex powered their way to eight wins in a row. Now they had to beat Surrey at Lord's in their last match to take the title. It was one of the greatest matches in the history of the County Championship, a game which saw the gates at Lord's closed twice, and a match which saw 'Plum' Warner play his last game for the county and steer them to the title in the most exciting circumstances.

Middlesex batted first and found themselves at 109 for five and struggling, before Warner and Stevens pulled them together with a stand of 90 for the seventh wicket. The following morning the Middlesex innings closed at 268 with Warner having made 79 and the nineteen-year-old Stevens 53. An undefeated 167 by Andrew Sandham enabled Surrey to declare at 341 for nine, a lead of 73. Lancashire were on the verge of beating Worcestershire and it looked as though the most Middlesex

> **Against Sussex at Lord's in 1920 the first four Middlesex batsmen scored centuries to create a world record. They were Warner (139), Lee (119), Hearne (118 not out) and Haig (131).**

could hope for was a draw, thus sending the Championship to Old Trafford. But the two Middlesex openers sensed that all was not lost. Harry Lee and the Oxford Blue, C. H. L. Skee, started slowly enough, adding 27 in the last three-quarters of an hour's play on the second day. But on the last day they let rip, taking the score to 208 inside three hours before Lee went for 108. Skeet followed soon after for 106. Then Middlesex chased runs and lost wickets rapidly. They were able to declare at 3.40pm with a score of 316 for seven. Warner had made 14 not out on his last

appearance at Lord's, adding 25 in only eight minutes with Stevens.

Surrey captain, P. G. H. Fender, thought that his side could score 244 in 180 minutes for victory. With the score at 22, Hobbs went, caught in the slips off a Nigel Haig outswinger after the catch had bounced out of Hendren's hands and into those of Lee. Stevens had Howell stumped by Murrell, but when Sandham and Shepherd took the score into three figures in only seventy-five minutes, it looked odds-on a Surrey victory. Then Stevens came back and had Tom Shepherd brilliantly caught in the deep by Hendren. Fender was bowled by Durston for a single and Middlesex's two leg-spinners now mopped up the Surrey's resistence.

Sandham and Peach staged a brief Surrey revival but the stage was now set for a remarkable Middlesex victory. Sandham was caught and bowled by Hearne and the Surrey resistance crumbled, although at one stage Sandham and Peach had taken them to within 101 of victory with one and a quarter hours left. When Stevens bowled Herbert Strudwick Middlesex had won by 55 runs with well over

The 1921 Champions: Back row left to right: R. H. Twinning, H. L. Dales, J. W. Hearne, F. Durston, A. R. Tanner, H. W. Lee. Front row: E. Hendren, N. Haig, F. T. Mann, Hon. C. N. Bruce, H. R. Murrell

half an hour to spare. Stevens had taken five for 61, Hearne three for 37, and Warner's last season had been marked by a Championship title.

The players who carried Middlesex to the Championship were led by Hendren with the bat and Hearne with the ball, though they were, naturally, well supported by many other players. Jack Durston had taken only five wickets for 74.20 runs each in his first season of 1919. Now he finished second to Hearne in the Middlesex averages with 111 wickets at around 20 runs apiece. Born in Bedfordshire, Durston came on to the Lord's ground staff in 1914 and with this first of two successive Middlesex Championships he burst upon the county scene. A tall, powerful man, Durston also played with Brentford as a goalkeeper for a spell. Behind Hearne and Durston, came Stevens with fourty-four Championship wickets in twelve games. Stevens narrowly missed the double in all games after a fine season at Oxford. Lee, Haig, Warner, Murrell and Mann were all invaluable in a good all-round team performance with 'Patsy' Hendren perhaps the most outstanding of an outstanding side. His 2,520 runs at 61.46 made him the best English batsman of 1920.

Frank Mann took over the captaincy in 1921 and guided Middlesex to a second successive Championship title, despite the fact that Stevens was not available for most of the season and 'Young Jack' Hearne suffered illness which reduced his effectiveness. Middlesex won their first eight matches and needed only to draw against Surrey to take the title. Surrey had to win to become champions and they had already beaten Middlesex by 19 runs at The Oval after a mammoth second innings effort by Middlesex, who reached 350, just failed to save the game. At Lord's Surrey led by 136 on their first innings, but Haig took five for 62 to bowl them out for 184 and Middlesex scored 322 for victory with time to spare, thanks to centuries from Hearne and Richard Twining who shared a stand of 277. Middlesex were champions again.

In this second Championship season of the Roaring Twenties Middlesex had a powerful batting side and against Nottinghamshire at Lord's they totalled 612 for eight with Lee making an undefeated 243.

Hearne, Hendren, Lee, Twining, Bruce and Mann, together with Haig and G. E. V. Crutchley, were all class batsmen. And if Hearne and Stevens could not contribute so much with the ball, then there were others who could. Haig took ninety-six wickets for Middlesex and there was solid support from Lee and Durston again. Middlesex were indeed worthy champions and, unlike 1920, there was never much doubt that they would finish top of the heap in 1921.

Although Hearne was back to fuller fitness and took more wickets, Middlesex slipped to seventh place in 1922. Mann had his best season with the bat, scoring 935 runs at 24.60 per innings for Middlesex and Hendren who had scored 277 not out against Kent at Lord's, had an average of over 75 runs. Hearne, as well as recovering his form with the ball, looked at one stage as though he would do the double, although he ultimately missed the feat this season. Haig and Durston supported him well with the ball and Durston did the hat-trick against Cambridge University at Fenners, finishing with six for 29. The previous summer his match analysis of eleven for 149 against Warwick Armstrong's Australian tourists resulted in his being chosen for the Second Test but, although he took five for 136 in the match, he was never chosen again. In 1922, D. R. Walker died, thus ending a hitherto unbroken link with the club since its formation. A. J. Webbe stepped up to become president.

Despite Hearne doing the double (and that after he missed the last seven games) and Hendren scoring well over 2,000 runs at an average of 87 per innings, Middlesex dropped a place to eighth in 1923. In all games Hendren passed 3,000 runs and headed the national averages. The greatest innings of that summer was Hearne's unbeaten 175 out of 289 on a difficult pitch against Yorkshire. Dales, Lee, Hearne and Hendren repeated the feat of the first four Middlesex batsmen scoring a century, this time against Hampshire. Haig bowled only a handful of overs through illness and the bowling as a whole was not as penetrative as previous seasons. The best win of the season was against Kent at Canterbury. In a high scoring first innings Kent made 445 (Woolley 270) and Middlesex 457. Kent went for 159 in their second innings and Middlesex got home by seven wickets.

In 1924 Middlesex went back to the higher reaches of the Championship and finished runners-up to Yorkshire who were in the middle of their great run of four successive Championships. They might have upset the Yorkshiremen's sequence had not Gloucestershire imposed a shock defeat on them. Durston and Haig rattled Gloucestershire out for 31 at Bristol before Middlesex themselves folded to 74 with Charlie Parker taking seven wickets. In their second innings Gloucestershire declared at 294 for four (with the twenty-one-year old Wally Hammond crashing Middlesex's bowlers all round the ground for an unbeaten 174) and then Parker claimed another seven wickets as Middlesex were all out for 190. Against Yorkshire at Lord's, Frank Mann hit Wilfred Rhodes for four 6s, including two which bounced off the roof of the pavilion.

When Nottinghamshire enforced the follow-on at Trent Bridge with Middlesex trailing by 209 runs, there were few, if any, on the ground who would have put

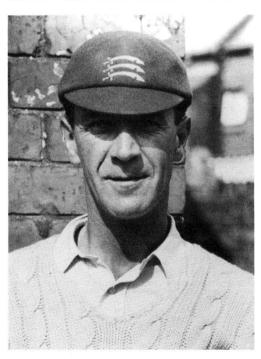

'Young Jack' Hearne. Despite ill-health he achieved the double of 1,000 runs and 100 wickets in a season four times for the club and was another in the great line of Middlesex all-rounders

money on a Middlesex victory. But in the second innings they reached 358 with John Guise scoring 100 before Nottinghamshire were bowled out for 122 with 'Gubby' Allen taking six for 31. Allen, who came to Middlesex from Cambridge University and who made his debut in 1921, was probably one of the fastest bowlers to ever wear the Middlesex sweater, despite a build not normally associated with pacemen. Stevens played more often, and with more success, and Haig was fit and back in harness. Although Hendren scored only 1,256 runs for Middlesex, his recall to the Test scene was highly successful and in all games he managed third place in the national averages. The amateur H. L. Dales enjoyed another good season.

In 1925 and 1926 Middlesex finished sixth in the Championship. In that first season Hendren enjoyed a prolific run-scoring fortnight with scores of 234, 37, 142, 240, 10 and 206 not out. Against Nottinghamshire his undefeated double century helped Middlesex to a sensational win when they scored 502 for six in their second innings to win the game. Bruce and Mann were also centurions in that match. There were big scores against too. Yorkshire's Percy Holmes made what was then the biggest-ever score at Lord's with 315 not out; and in the game at Headingley, Leyland and Sutcliffe opened with a stand of 218 and Sutcliffe went on to score 235 off the Middlesex attack. Throughout the season the Middlesex batting was supported by Stevens and Hearne, and the bowling saw the usual trio of Hearne, Haig and Durston head the field. E. J. North took thirty-four wickets and Walter Robins, still at school, started with Middlesex. Robins was scheduled for a Cambridge Blue in 1926 and H. J. Enthoven, also of Cambridge, began his Middlesex career in the same season as Robins.

Moderate bowling saw Middlesex again finish sixth the following season with Hearne turning in only occasional flashes of brilliance and Durston now nearing the retirement age for pacemen. Hearne's best performance of the season was five wickets against Nottinghamshire who failed to score 196 to win; and a measure of the poor penetrative quality of the Middlesex attack was that Jack Hobbs made 316 not out against them and so broke the highest-ever innings played at Lord's which had stood for only one year.

It was the batting which saved Middlesex so often and at Edgbaston where Frank Mann made 194 to save the game after Warwickshire took a first-innings lead of over 200. Middlesex were weakened by the loss of Hendren, Stevens and Hearne that day and slow-left-arm bowler George Paine took eight wickets. It impressed Warwickshire so much that he eventually qualified for them and went on to become one of their leading bowlers. It was yet another example of a fine player who Middlesex let slip due to the practice of playing the amateurs whenever they were available, thus stunting the progress of young professionals like Paine.

Hendren's 213 against Yorkshire at Lord's was his highest-ever score that summer and he made 1,707 runs for Middlesex, 1,639 of them in the Championship. Hearne made 1,111 Championship runs at an average of around 55, and Stevens, Mann and Bruce were the other main run-getters. Hendren missed seven Championship games through the Tests and Stevens found himself in the England side for the last two games against Australia, thanks, undoubtedly, to a fine

performance when the tourists came to Lord's for the county match. 'Gubby' Allen captured the last four Australian wickets in less than two overs and the tourists finished with 489. Middlesex looked likely to follow-on but Stevens who opened, scored 149 and held the innings together. When his wicket — the ninth — finally fell, Stevens had averted the danger for Middlesex and caught the eyes of the Test selectors.

Middlesex finished ninth in 1927 after drawing fourteen Championship games and winning only five in a mostly damp season. Hendren, despite the conditions, romped on with the bat, scoring 2,033 runs for Middlesex and over 2,700 in all games to finish fourth in the English averages with over 73 runs per innings. He scored eight centuries for Middlesex, thirteen altogether, and made 201 not out against Essex at Leyton. Hearne started in tremendous fashion with 245 not out against Gloucestershire at Bristol, an innings which helped him on the way to 750 runs in May.

No bowler managed 100 Championship wickets for Middlesex and, in fact, Middlesex had bad luck with their attack because Durston was injured for much of the season and Allen and Stevens played little cricket. Fred Price took over from Murrell behind the stumps with the former wicketkeeper retiring at the end of 1926 with 777 victims (517 caught and 260 stumped) in his career at Lord's. In his final season of 1926 he had six in an innings against Gloucestershire at Bristol (four caught and two stumped).

Nigel Haig took over the Middlesex captaincy in 1929

Against Lancashire at Lord's in 1927, H. J. Enthoven had taken well over two hours to reach 50 as Middlesex struggled to avoid the follow-on. With only two wickets left they still needed 55 to make Lancashire bat again when Enthoven suddenly opened his shoulders and scored another 89 runs in less than an hour.

The county moved up to eighth spot in 1928 with Hendren having an even better season with the bat. In all games, his aggregate rose to 3,311 runs, 2,623 of which were for Middlesex, with 2,471 runs in the Championship alone. He hit eleven centuries for the county, thirteen in all, and again his average was over 70 which gave him fourth place in the English national averages. But if Hendren lifted Middlesex's fortunes up, then injury still dogged the attack and Hearne was injured when fielding a fierce full-blooded shot from Learie Constantine when the West Indian tourists came to Lord's. 'Young Jack' was doing well with both ball and bat — with nearly 700 runs in his first eight Championship matches — when that injury put him out for the rest of the season. Allen played only twice and with Stevens failing to register a single game. Middlesex were still a talented side, but suffering from some ill-luck which prevented them from climbing back to the top of the Championship.

Haig was now Middlesex skipper and he led from the front, doing the double and opening both batting and bowling. Hendren did not do so well as the previous two seasons, losing his place in the Test side after the Fourth Test against South Africa, although we must remember we are judging his 1929 season by his own remarkable standards. Middlesex finished in sixth place, winning twelve and drawing nine of their twenty-eight Championship games. Two years earlier, Hendren had scored a double century at Leyton. Now it was Hearne's turn with 285 not out against Essex on the same ground. It was Middlesex's highest individual score until Hendren beat it at Dudley in 1933.

Ian Peebles arrived on the scene as a leg-spinner and took 100 wickets in his first full season, and Haig and Robins were also into three figures. Robins did the hat-trick against Leicestershire at Lord's; and Allen took ten for 40 against Lancashire at Lord's and then hit a splendid century at The Oval. Robins had a fine season, doing the double for the only time in his career and playing in the Second Test. Cambridge University player, Tom Killick, played twice for England.

The continual changing of the Middlesex team, due to players being unavailable through representative calls, university, and injuries, led Middlesex to sixteenth place in 1930, only a whisker above bottom club Nottinghamshire. Middlesex had still not recorded their first win after twenty games when Peebles returned from Oxford and helped Middlesex to win three of their last eight games. He topped the bowling averages with forty-four wickets at less than 11 runs apiece. Although the leading wicket-takers were Hearne, Durston and Haig, they were all expensive and Allen went second in the averages with twenty-six wickets at under 18 runs each. Durston was now slowing down and making more contributions with the bat than the ball. Haig was over forty and Hearne, too, was well into the veteran stage.

Hendren, Hearne and Lee led the batsmen, though all with reduced averages, and Arsenal footballer, Joe Hulme, made his maiden century at Edgbaston. Robins was playing cricket with Sir Julian Cahn's team and Allen was available occasionally, though doing enough with the ball to more than justify his selection. But overall 1930 was a hard slog for Middlesex.

Although 1931 was also a dreadfully wet summer, Middlesex pulled up to eleventh place after winning four of their first six championship games. Alas, the next Middlesex victory did not come until the very last game of the season against bottom-of-the-table Northamptonshire. In the batting Hendren and Hearne led the way with Stevens, who was now regularly available, finishing third in the averages. Hendren was way out in front with an average of over 60; Hearne and Stevens each had averages of half that figure.

Peebles was also available regularly and he was the leading wicket-taker with 100 at 17.35 each for Championship matches. He had match figures of eleven for 130 against Glamorgan, eleven for 124 against Essex, and ten for 107 against Somerset. In the Glamorgan game Hearne was in tremendous form with the bat and scored centuries in both innings when the two counties met for the first time. Only Durston, who now bowled off-breaks, supported Peebles to any great extent and Haig, Stevens and Hearne all had expensive seasons. For Hendren, in another fine season with the bat, a second benefit match against Sussex was rewarded with a century. He made over 2,000 Championship runs in 1931.

Middlesex won four of their first ten matches in 1932, but only two more victories in the rest of the season saw them finish in tenth place. While the batting was again excellent — Hendren and Hearne both scored over 2,000 runs in all first-class matches — the bowling was letting Middlesex down once more. Although Durston took 106 wickets in all games for Middlesex, and despite the fact that Peebles had seventy-two victims in sixteen Championship matches (including a hat-trick against Gloucestershire at Lord's), the others did badly. Haig and the rest of the bowlers, including Hearne and Enthoven, were all capable of only ordinary performances. The only remotely successful player, besides Durston and Peebles, was the leg-spinner, J. M. Sims, who started with Middlesex in 1929 and who took forty-one wickets in 1932 and who also weighed in with a century against Surrey at The Oval.

It was a high-scoring summer. Hulme took his chance and passed 1,000 runs for the first time and Sims's century against Surrey at The Oval was just part of an exceptionally fine cricket match. Middlesex were all out for 141 in their first innings before Surrey declared at a massive 540 for nine with Freddie Brown (212) and Douglas Jardine (126) murdering the Middlesex bowling. Then it was Middlesex's turn. Hendren made 145 and Sims, who opened the innings, 103. They

helped Middlesex on the way to 455, leaving Surrey to get 57 in about twenty minutes. With three balls left, Surrey needed ten more runs and had lost four wickets. Durston's fourth ball of the last over was driven for two by Jardine, although the Surrey batsman was dropped at deep mid-off. The penultimate ball found its way through the slips for four. And the last ball was driven straight to see Surrey home in a most remarkable match.

That was Haig's last season in sole charge. For 1933 and 1934 he shared the captaincy with all-rounder H. J. Enthoven, who made his first-class debut for Middlesex in 1925. In those seasons of shared captaincy, Middlesex finished in twelfth place in 1933 and tenth in 1934. In 1933 Hendren made nearly 2,500 runs in the Championship and over 3,000 in all first-class games for the third time. In the Championship he headed the averages with over 63 runs per innings, followed by Hearne and Hulme who were way behind him. At Dudley, Hendren made his highest ever score, 301 not out against Worcestershire in seven hours. It was the highest score ever made by a Middlesex batsman

Nigel Haig is caught in the slips against Surrey at The Oval in 1934

for the county, eclipsing J. W. Hearne's 285 not out against Essex at Leyton four years earlier. Hendren also scored over 1,000 of his runs in August alone. Again, though, the bowling was indifferent and Hearne's fifty-three wickets were the highest of any Middlesex Championship bowler.

In 1934, it was the emergence of a young Wiltshire bowler, Jim Smith, who did much to lift the hearts of Middlesex supporters. Smith took 139 Championship wickets in his first full season, 143 in all games for the county that season, and 172 in every first-class game he played to finish high in the national averages with figures of 18.88 apiece. Cedric Ivan James Smith, always known as 'Big Jim', had been on the staff at Lord's since 1926. He stood six feet four inches and that winter played in all the Tests against the West Indies, despite his lack of first-class experience. Apart from his bowling 'Big Jim' was also a fearsome hitter of the ball and against Gloucestershire at Bristol in 1938 he hit 50 in only eleven minutes! Joe Hulme had a good 1934 season with both bat and ball, scoring 1,258 which was a higher Championship figure than any other Middlesex player, although he finished behind Hendren in the averages. Hendren played in four Tests against Australia while Fred Price was the only other man to score 1,000 Championship runs for the county.

In the five seasons before cricket closed down for the duration of World War II, Middlesex finished third in 1935 and then runners-up for the next four consecutive seasons. Robins took over the captaincy from Haig and Enthoven, and the new skipper enjoyed the luxuries which his predecessors had not. Besides the new bowling sensation Jim Smith, he had Allen available more often, and with himself, and early in the 1935 season, Peebles to follow up with spin, Robins had a formidable attack with which to test Yorkshire for the Championship. In addition, Sims came through to the extent that he was the only Middlesex bowler to take 100 Championship wickets. Hendren was his usual immaculate self with the bat and he scored 1,688 in all games for the county, 1,649 coming in the Championship at 51.50 per innings. John Human and the South African, J. G. Owen-Smith both

added weight to the batting, and Sims had a splendid match against Surrey at Lord's with 53 and 25 not out, and match figures of nine for 97, although rain prevented a result. Meanwhile, in the Middlesex Second Eleven which won the Minor Counties title at the first attempt were Jack Young, Jack Robertson — and Denis Compton.

In 1936, when they began their four consecutive seasons of finishing runners-up, the Middlesex batting averages made interesting reading. For the first time since before World War I, Hendren was not top. His place went to Allen who played in less than a dozen games and averaged 50 with the bat. Hendren was

'Gubby' Allen in action

'Patsy' Hendren and Denis Compton going out to bat at The Oval in 1936. Their careers overlapped by just two seasons

not far behind and Denis Compton and Joe Hulme, who hit 1,000 runs, followed, Middlesex lost their first two games but picked up to win ten Championship games as well as defeat the Indians. The bowling was spearheaded again by Smith, with Sims (who had match figures of ten for 106 against Surrey at The Oval), Robins, Laurie Gray (a fast-medium seamer) and Allen giving able support. Peebles played in half the games but took only twenty-five reasonably expensive wickets. Only in the opening batting spot did Middlesex have a problem where Price, though he deserved the chance, had not come off. The Championship went to Derbyshire, their single honour until they won the Nat West Trophy in 1981, and Middlesex never really looked like topping them.

The 1937 season was 'Patsy' Hendren's last. At the age of forty-eight he was still going strong and only Bill Edrich, having qualified from Norfolk, topped the old master's Championship aggregate of 1,380 runs. Although his very last innings at Lord's, against Surrey, saw him register a duck, Hendren had made a century in the first innings. His career figures are phenomenal — 40,302 runs for Middlesex, with an average of 48.82, and in all first-class cricket, 57,610 runs at 50.80 per innings. He hit 119 centuries for Middlesex alone and 170 in all games. Only Sir Jack Hobbs scored more centuries; only Hobbs and Frank Woolley more runs. Hendren, Edrich, Compton led the Middlesex batting in 1937; Smith, Sims, Gray, Robins and Owen-Smith were the attack for most of the season. Denis Compton made all but 2,000 runs in all games in only his second season, while Edrich, in his first full term, did top the 2,000 mark. Middlesex won fifteen of their twenty-four Championship games. Yorkshire won eighteen of their twenty-eight and took the title with a better points average. In a special challenge match at the season's end, Yorkshire beat Middlesex by an innings and 115 runs to underline their superiority.

In 1938 Middlesex again won fifteen out of twenty-four matches and finished second, although they lost one more game, making five in all, while Yorkshire again won the title in this, one of their vintage periods. Bill Edrich led the way with the bat, scoring 1,675 Championship runs at 64.42 per innings, with Denis Compton second. Compton also passed 1,000 runs — he and Edrich were the only Middlesex players to reach that target — but Compton's average was some ten runs inferior to that

Middlesex skipper Walter Robins is caught by Wade off Smith during the run chase at Chelmsford in 1938. Middlesex needed 224 to beat Essex on the last day and got home with one wicket to spare

of Edrich, although it was still a fine record. Both men played in all five Test Matches against Australia. There was the pleasing sight of newcomers, Sid Brown and Jack Robertson both doing well with the bat. Brown scored a century at Old Trafford that season, while Robertson made an impressive start with 81 in his first innings, against Surrey at Lord's.

The same match and Bill Edrich makes a fine one-handed catch to remove Gregory

With Brown and Robertson to share the opening spot with Edrich, Middlesex's batting looked even more secure. Edrich, Compton and Robertson led the averages. Smith took over 100 Championship wickets, and with Gray and Robins in good form, and Peebles back to something like his former self, the Middlesex attack was an admirable foil to the county's batting strength.

Edrich made 1,000 runs by the end of May, although he only just achieved the feat. A magnificent 245 against Nottingham at Lord's took him to within 19 runs of his target. But then the rain intervened;

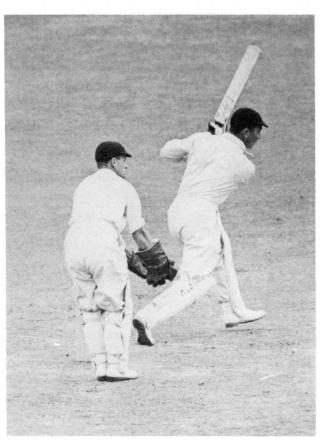

Denis Compton drives Notts' Arthur Jepson through the covers in July 1939. It was an historic match for Middlesex who were playing a home game at The Oval due to Lord's being needed for a public schools match.

The summer of 1939 was one of high tension throughout Europe and the cricket season was played in an unreal atmosphere. Robins resigned as Middlesex skipper and his place was taken by Peebles. Middlesex again finished runners-up to Yorkshire and when the sides met at Lord's, the Tykes underlined their superiority with an overwhelming win. They made 430 for five declared (Leyland 180 not out, Sutcliffe 175), and then bowled out Middlesex for 62 and 122, although it must be said that the home side had much the worse of the conditions. Throughout the season, Middlesex's batting rested on the shoulders of Compton, Edrich and Robertson. Compton and Edrich both topped 2,000 runs in all games, Robertson over 1,700. The rest came nowhere by comparison. Sims climbed back to top form with the ball, taking 142 Championship wickets, and Smith had eighty-four. Again, the rest were also-rans. Smith also managed his only first-class century with 101 not out at Canterbury. He scored 98 of 116 added with Peebles for the last wicket. It took just eighty-one minutes and *Wisden* commented that, compared with his normal efforts it was quite a sedate performance!

When Middlesex met Nottinghamshire that season, the home game was played at The Oval because Lord's was needed for a public school match. It was a disaster for Middlesex. W. W. Keeton scored a record 312 not out for Nottinghamshire and they declared at 560 for nine before Voce, with seven wickets, helped bowl out Middlesex for 119 to win the match for the Midlanders. To balance the record Middlesex won by ten wickets at Trent Bridge where Edrich made 160. But the season was drawing to an unhappy close. In the last game to be played, Robertson and Edrich each scored centuries as Middlesex reached 525 for seven declared against Warwickshire. Then Sims took eight wickets, Warwickshire were bowled out twice and the game finished with a day in hand. But war was near. The West Indians curtailed their tour and the Middlesex match against Kent, due to start on the eve of war, was cancelled. Many careers would suffer because of the six-year break, including those of Sims and Robertson. And who knows what records Compton and Edrich might have broken, but for Hitler?

against Worcestershire he failed to score when Middlesex won by an innings, and when rain washed out the first day's play against the Australians, and when he made only 9 in the Middlesex first innings against the tourists, it looked as though Edrich would be robbed of his chance. But Don Bradman, who had beaten Edrich to 1,000 runs in that game, declared, and with about 30 minutes remaining Edrich reached his target in what was, by then, an otherwise meaningless knock. With Edrich and Compton selected for all the Tests, Middlesex gained a further honour when Fred Price kept wicket at Headingley. It was an inauspicious England debut, however. England lost, to go one down in the series, and Price saw Bradman make his third successive Test hundred. The Middlesex wicketkeeper batted at number seven but made 0 to 6. It was his only appearance for England.

Runs Galore

Middlesex began the 1946 season — the first since the war — in the happy position of having three class batsmen in Compton, Edrich and Robertson still at the very height of their powers. Like soccer, county cricket had lost a lot of experienced players between 1939 and 1945, either through the tragedies of enemy action, or simply through the advancing years which had seen them grow old before sport was resumed in peacetime. Cricket was a mixture of experience and raw talent. But Middlesex, though they lacked the former in their pace attack, had an abundance of players who remained to strike runs in those early post-war campagns. Besides the trio mentioned above, there was also Sid Brown, who had blossomed into a fine opening partner for Robertson. The side was captained by Walter Robins, who, at the age of forty, had decided to make himself regularly available once more. Jim Sims, aged forty-two, was also still at Lord's, and so too was Fred Price who, at forty-four, had been recalled from intended retirement to keep wicket after his replacement, the amateur C. R. N. Maxwell, failed to live up to expectations and played in only seven games.

One player who had retired was Jim Smith and his place took some filling. Indeed, it was not until the emergence of Alan Moss in 1950 that the gap was properly plugged. With Smith gone, the new-ball attack was left to Bill Edrich and Laurie Gray, though neither would have claimed to be first-line bowlers. Robins bowled leg-spins, although the advance of years made him much less effective, and there was little Jack Young, the left-arm spinner, and Sims. The first season saw Middlesex finish second, once again to Yorkshire. They won sixteen of their twenty-six games and the rest were equally divided between defeats and draws. Yorkshire took the top spot by twelve points. Middlesex won seven of their last nine games. One more win and they would

have tied with the champions. Robertson showed his class in the match against Kent at Lord's where he scored 104 out of 242 on a difficult pitch. A thunderstorm gave Kent the conditions to win by an innings after the visitors' first three batsmen had scored centuries.

Towards the end of 1946 the Middlesex batsmen were in full swing. In the penultimate game of the season Compton hit 235 against Surrey at Lord's and with Edrich (147) put on 269 at well over a run a minute. And in the last game, against Essex, Robins and Thompson added 191 in only ninety minutes, with Robins scor-

Denis Compton reaches his double century for Middlesex against The Rest at The Oval in 1947

ing a whirlwind 102. That merry run chase was carried on into the scorching summer of 1947 (which followed one of the worst winter s in memory when Compton's Arsenal were still playing at Highbury at the end of May). Runs just sizzled of the bats of Compton, Edrich and company. Compton and Edrich both passed the previous record aggregate of runs in one season, and their massive accumulation continued right up until the final game of the season when, as champion county, Middlesex beat a powerful Rest team by nine wickets. Compton made 246, despite an injured knee, and Edrich 180. Middlesex declared at 543 for nine and then The Rest made 246 and, following-on, 317. Middlesex scored the runs they needed to cap a magnificent season for the loss of just one wicket.

Besides Compton and Edrich, however, there were other Middlesex batsmen who, if their efforts did not reach the epic proportions of the 'twins', certainly went a long way towards bolstering the Championship challenge. Brown and Robertson shared nine opening stands of 100 or more, and in the Nottinghamshire match at Lord's they made 310 for the first wicket to create a new Middlesex record. There was also support from a most unexpected quarter. Alan Fairbairn, a left-hander who played for Southgate, came into the side and made centuries in his first two county innings. Fairbairn was also involved in one of those eccentric incidents which help to make cricket such a fascinating game.

When Middlesex went to Derby in August 1947, they faced a Derbyshire attack depleted by Test calls to Bill Copson and Cliff Gladwin, In their second innings Middlesex had a lead of 27 and Brown and Fairbairn set about consolidating that position. Then came the bowling feat of the season.

Derbyshire were captained at that time by Eddie Gothard, forty-two years old and a gentle man who played with his spectacles adhered to his temples with sticking plaster. Gothard played with Staffordshire in the Minor Counties Competition. But not even his best friends regarded him as a first-class cricketer, charming man though he was. He bowled gentle seamers and, after Pope, Rhodes and Worthington had been hit all round

the ground, the Derbyshire skipper put himself on to bowl and soon found Brown and Fairbairn treating his bowling with similar contempt. Then, the unthinkable happened. Gothard had Fairbairn caught by Rhodes, dismissed Edrich, caught and bowled with the next delivery, and had a furious Walter Robins taken off a defensive prod to complete one of the most unlikely hat-tricks in first-class cricket! It was a feat which took Gothard's first-class wickets haul to six, although the following season this likable cricketer performed his second great bowling feat by clean bowling Don Bradman at Derby. Despite some red faces in that 1947 game, however, Middlesex got home quite easily and stayed on course for the Championship.

Denis Compton's brother, Leslie, who had taken over the wicketkeeping duties, scored a century after the hat-trick at Derby and George Mann, son of Frank, also scored a century. Those two and Fairbairn hit four centuries between them. The other thirty-three scored by Middlesex batsmen in 1947 were shared by Denis Compton, Edrich, Robertson and Brown. One of the most exciting wins was at Leicester where the home county were 17 runs ahead with four wickets lost on the last afternoon. Then Middlesex struck and the last six men were out in just over half an hour for 48 runs. Edrich and Compton scored the 66 needed to win in only seven overs with less than five minutes to spare. Gloucestershire pushed Middlesex hard for Championship and the crunch came at Cheltenham in mid-August. Denis Compton and Robertson were playing in the Test and Edrich was barely fit for the match at Cheltenham through a shoulder injury. Middlesex made 180, Gloucestershire 153, and in Middlesex's second innings they were 33 for two when Harry Sharp took over to steer his side through.

In 1947 the Middlesex run machine's first four batsmen — Compton, Edrich, Robertson ai·d Brown — scored an aggregate of over 12,000 in all first-class games.

Sharp had top score with 46 and Middlesex managed to reach a reasonable second innings figure and set Gloucestershire 169 for victory. Again, Sharp played his part. It was his first game of the season and after his sterling efforts with the bat, he took three wickets to break the back of the Gloucestershire innings. Young and Sims did the rest and Gloucestershire were dismissed for 100 runs to leave but he was a far better batsman than many who have earned more England Test honours.

But let us not forget the Middlesex bowlers in 1947. Jack Young took 122 Championship wickets at 15.81 each and in all games for the county he bagged 139. Sims, despite being sidelined through injury for a spell, took 120 in all Middlesex matches. And Gray (eighty-four) and

Bill Edrich joined Compton in his record-breaking spree of 1947

Fast bowler John Warr made his debut for Middlesex in 1949

Middlesex in a commanding position. In this Championship-winning season Compton scored a record 3,816 runs in all games at an average of 90.85 with eighteen centuries. Edrich also passed the old record — set by Surrey's Tom Hayward who scored 3,518 in 1906 — and made 3,539 in all games, averaging 80.43

Robertson had 2,760 runs and Brown 2,078. For Middlesex alone, it was Edrich who had the record with 2,650 at 84.48, while Compton's county aggregate was 2,467 at an average of102.79. Robertson had 2,328 for Middlesex (average 55.43) and Brown was just 10 runs short of 2,000 for Middlesex. Robertson should have played more times for England. The selectors begrudgingly gave him eleven caps

Denis Compton (fifty-seven) were also valuable wicket-takers. A newcomer was Ian Bedford who burst on the scene by taking six for 134 in the match against Essex at Lord's in his first Championship game and ended the season second to Young in the averages with twenty-five wickets at less than 20 runs each. Bedford was only seventeen and still at Woodhouse Grammar School when he came through to the first-class game with his leg-spinners and googlies. This was to be his best season and after service in the RAF he went back to club cricket before being recalled to lead Middlesex after John Warr retired. Sadly, he died in September 1966 after collapsing while batting for Finchley at Buckhurst Hill, a far cry from the fury of this Middlesex Championship-winning campaign.

In 1948 Middlesex failed to retain the title which went to Glamorgan, the first time that the Welsh county had finished top of the Championship. Middlesex finished third, behind Surrey, and new captain George Mann's task was made difficult by the loss of Denis Compton, Edrich and Young for the Tests against Australia. Middlesex won their first four games, succeeding thirteen times in all, but Glamorgan's success in taking first-innings points on three occasions more than Middlesex, ensured that they finished on top. Robertson was the highest Middlesex run-getter with 1,855 in the Championship and 1,951 in all game for the county. Compton and Edrich were top of the averages, each with an average of over 60 (Robertson's was nearly 55) and Brown made 1,249 in all Middlesex matches. There was sterling support from John Dewes, an uncomplicated batsman who found himself catapulted into the last Test where he made 1 and 10 against Miller and Lindwall, and from Sharp, Leslie Compton, Mann, Thompson and Robins. Against Somerset at Lord's, Denis Compton (252 not out) and Edrich (168 not out) set up a record unfinished third-wicket stand of 424. Young took ninety-three wickets and Sims and Gray supported him well.

But Middlesex were still short of a really penetrative pace attack and in 1949, as they went back to the top to share the Championship with Yorkshire, the emergence of the Cambridge Blue, John Warr, helped Middlesex to put in a late challenge for an outright title win. The last match was against Derbyshire and Warr's five for 36 went a long way to ensuring that Middlesex had at least one hand on the Championship. The New

Zealanders had to make do with four three-day Tests, which meant that Middlesex had their international players available more often.

Until August, Middlesex were undefeated but a double defeat at the hands of Surrey, and a slip against Sussex at Hove, denied them an outright title. Compton, Edrich, Robertson, Brown, Sharp, Thompson and the rest of the Middlesex batting line-up continued to power the runs with the first three all scoring over 2,000 runs in all games. The most outstanding piece of batting came at Worcester where Robertson scored an undefeated 331, still the highest score ever made for Middlesex. Robertson's runs came in six and half hours and Middlesex declared at 623 for five.

Warr's arrival — he took thirty wickets for Middlesex after the end of the Cambridge season — eased the burden on the other bowlers. Jack Young took 131 wickets in all Middlesex games, Sims 126, and Gray sixty. The others contributed little — or if they did it was at an expensive cost — although Allen, now aged forty-seven, managed thirteen economical wickets. One young player who slipped in almost unnoticed was Fred Titmus. His contribution was insignificant in 1949 and gave no hint of the great all-rounder he would become.

The end of the 1949 season marked the end of Middlesex as Championship challengers for more than two decades. George Mann resigned the captaincy and, although Robins took over for 1950, he played only ten games and Middlesex found themselves with a different skipper in almost every game. At various times, Denis Compton, Edrich, Mann, Allen, Sims and Dewes all tried their hand at one of the the most difficult jobs in sport. This had an obvious effect on the side's performance and from joint top in 1949, Middlesex went down to fourteenth place in 1950.

In 1950 Middlesex were also handicapped by the loss, for large parts of the season, of Compton and Edrich, through Test calls and injuries. Robertson and Sharp were the main run-getters, Robertson scoring 1,901 in all Middlesex games, and Sharp 1,328. Young and Sims were again the main-line bowlers until Warr ended his university season, and Gray

---

When Middlesex were set to make 206 in two hours and ten minutes against Kent at Lord's in 1948, an exciting finish looked in prospect. With three balls left, Middlesex needed three runs; Kent needed to take one wicket for victory. Gray played Ridgeway's last three balls safely and the result was a draw.

J. G. Dewes hits a 6 off Surrey at The Oval in 1951

was down to thirty-seven victims. Titmus was on the way up, however, and he claimed forty-five wickets. Sixteen-year-old pace bowler, Don Bennett, and Alan Moss made their first appearances in 1950. In 1951, Denis Compton and Edrich shared the captaincy as Middlesex climbed to seventh place. Highlight of that season was an innings of 232 not out by Brown against Somerset at Lord's. It was Brown's last good season. He scored almost 1,700 runs in all games (1,498 of them for the county) and made 194 at Portsmouth when he and Robertson (135) added 232 for the first wicket. But Robertson was again the leading runmaker. He made 2,542 Championship runs, 2,622 in all Middlesex games (second only to Edrich's 1947 record), and 2,917 in every

first class game in which he played. He became the first batsman to pass 2,000 runs that season, during his 201 not out against Somerset at Taunton on 17 July.

Middlesex cricket, indeed, all cricket, was passing into a new age. The club which had depended so much on the uninhibited talent of some great amateur batsmen, would now have to readjust to the ultra-professional game which cricket was ultimately to become. The days when amateurs could take up their places in the county side during the school and university holidays were drawing swiftly to a close. Although the line between 'Gentlemen' and 'Players' would continue to be drawn for some time to come, Middlesex cricket would have a new look about it as it moved into a new Elizabethan age.

1952

Out of Touch

Middlesex 1952: Back row left to right: Bennett, Sharp, Moss, L. Compton, Warr, Brown, Thompson. Front row: Robertson, D. Compton, Edrich, Young, Knightley-Smith.

Middlesex's season fell very distinctly into two sections. In the first fourteen Championship games they took 120 points with ten victories and stood second in the table; in the last fourteen they could only manage a paltry sixteen points and were lucky to finish as high a fifth. But even their early good form, which had Middlesex supporters thinking about the Championship, was not reflective of the side's overall ability. *Wisden* commented: 'Undoubtedly, Middlesex were never as strong as their early record suggested. Several times their chance of victory resulted chiefly from the desire of both captains to provide a definite finish.'

For sure, the Middlesex batsmen were sadly out of touch for much of the season, Denis Compton's own batting fell away during the latter half of the summer, although he still collected 1,439 for the county alone (averaging 36.89) and weighed in with seventy-four wickets. *Wisden*

made the observation that many cricketers would rejoice if, like Compton, they came near the double of 2,000 runs and 100 wickets in all matches. Yet judged by his own incomparable standards, the man had failed during the Middlesex demise of July and August. Jack Robertson also had a relatively poor second half of the season, although he maintained his record of being the only post-war batsman to have scored 2,000 runs every season since peace was restored.

The other batsmen had mixed fortunes. Bill Edrich, returning after an injury, scored four centuries for Middlesex, including a sparkling unbeaten 175 against Worcestershire at Worcester where he shared in a second-wicket stand of 315 with Alec Thompson (158). But even Edrich was inconsistent and his second place in the county averages owed much to the occasional brilliant innings rather than an overall run of solid knocks. Sid

Brown disappointed and Harry Sharp was another man who failed to score regularly over the season, although he played in only half the games. Some useful runs came from the amateur W. Knightley-Smith who was awarded his Middlesex cap.

> **At Lord's on 30 June 1952 Middlesex were struggling at 215 for eight in reply to Hampshire's 298 when seventeen-year-old reserve wicketkeeper John Murray took over and hit his first half-century in first-class cricket. Young helped him to add 82 for the ninth wicket and Denis Compton was able to declare one run ahead. Middlesex needed 197 at 90 an hour to win the game and got them with three wickets and five minutes to spare, thanks to a fine 86 not out by Sid Brown.**

In the Middlesex bowling department there was a brighter story. Despite being handicapped by knee trouble, Jack Young took 137 Championship wickets and topped the averages at a cost of 20.47 each. But the brightest part of the story was the arrival of Alan Moss for his first full season. Moss took eighty-eight wickets for Middlesex alone and ninety-five in all first-class matches. Don Bennett took thirty-three wickets in his twenty-one games and the eccentric left-arm slows of Denis Compton accounted, as we have seen, for many valuable wickets. Too often in 1952 Middlesex bowlers had only small targets at which to bowl, thanks to the poor showing of their batsmen. They applied themselves splendidly and but, for the attack, the fortunes of Middlesex CCC might have taken an even more abrupt downturn.

Middlesex's game against the Indian tourists in 1952 goes down in the statistics as a draw, but it gave Lord's followers some interesting and entertaining cricket. India's first innings was one of fits and starts and it reached 289, thanks only to some marvellous batting by Manjrekar, who hit fifteen 4s in his 104. When Middlesex batted Jack Robertson gave a similarly entertaining display with 85 before he was trapped leg-before by Divecha. Then the Indian skipper Hazare took four wickets for three runs in eight balls and Middlesex's middle order collapsed. They were all out for 255, with some stout batting by John Warr who made 35 not out, and Hazare finished with seven for 50.

Thanks to a brilliant stand of 168 in 105 minutes by Roy (131) and Umrigar (86), Hazare was able to declare before lunch on the last day and set Middlesex 329 in

Denis Compton turns the ball past Surridge and Parker of Surrey at The Oval

four hours to win the match. They started slowly after losing Sharp for a duck with only three runs on the board, and it was not until Denis Compton and Bill Edrich came together that a victory looked possible. Edrich scored a fine 129 and Compton made 70 before they were both out to Hazare. When Knightley-Smith was caught by Phadkar off Divecha for 0, Middlesex called off their chase with 40 runs still needed and the game into the last half-hour which Middlesex had claimed.

FIRST CLASS RESULTS 1952
Championship Record

P	W	L	D	No Dcsn	Pos
28	11	12	4	1	5th

May

7-9	beat Derbyshire by nine wickets at Lord's
10-13	lost to Glamorgan by 131 runs at Lord's
14-16	beat Worcestershire by 31 runs at Lord's
17-20	beat Northants by 46 runs at Northampton
21-3	beat Gloucestershire by 111 runs at Lord's
24-7	lost to Leicestershire by seven wickets at Leicester

May 31, **June** 2, 3 beat Sussex by 70 runs at Lord's

June

4-6	drew with Cambridge University at Fenners
7-10	beat Kent by 46 runs at Lord's
11-13	beat Northants by 23 runs at Lord's
14-16	drew with Yorkshire at Lord's
18-20	beat Oxford University by 49 runs at The Parks
21-4	lost to Somerset by 54 runs at Bath
25-7	beat Gloucestershire by 71 runs at Gloucester

June 28, 30 **July** 1 beat Hampshire by three wickets at Lord's

July

2-3	beat Worcestershire by nine wickets at Dudley
5-8	drew with Essex at Colchester
12-15	drew with Lancashire at Old Trafford
16-18	lost to Derbyshire by 52 runs at Derby
19-22	lost to Surrey by nine wickets at Lord's
23-5	drew with Nottinghamshire at Trent Bridge
26-9	lost to Yorkshire by ten wickets at Sheffield

August

2-5	lost to Sussex by 15 runs at Hove
6-8	lost to Hampshire by an innings and 25 runs at Portsmouth
9-12	lost to Surrey by eight wickets at The Oval
13-15	beat Kent by 27 runs at Dover
16-19	no decision in the match with Nottinghamshire at Lord's
20-2	lost to Essex by 111 runs at Lord's
23-6	drew with the Indians at Lord's
27-9	lost to Warwickshire by 72 runs at Lord's

August 30, **September** 1, 2 lost to Lancashire by nine wickets at Lord's

1953

Titmus Arrives

Yet again Middlesex started the season in splendid fashion and then fell away badly to finish in fifth place after leading the Championship for part of the summer. This time, however, there were good reasons for this second-half failure. Denis Compton came back to form and regained his England place, which meant, of course, that Middlesex had to manage without him when the Tests were played. Compton missed thirteen Championship games, either through representitive calls or his knee injury which caused him problems throughout 1953. Compton played in all five Tests against Australia and Bill Edrich was called up for three, so he, too, missed some vital Middlesex matches. Edrich now had sole captaincy of the side this season after sharing the job with Denis Compton.

The season had started in somewhat sensational fashion with a tied game at Peterborough, only the fourteenth such result in first-class cricket since World War I. Thanks to an innings of exactly 100 by Denis Compton, Northants were set to score 227 to win. Alan Moss set about the Northants batting and when the eighth wicket fell he had taken five of them and Northants still needed two runs to win. With the scores level Leslie Compton stumped Starkie off Young with poor Barrick stranded at the other end, 80 not out, and then Young uprooted Fiddling's off stump and the two sides shared twelve points, the match being the first to be decided under the new points rule for tied matches.

Middlesex were unlucky to lose Jack Robertson for eight Championship games.

Edrich drives Hampshire's Cannings for a single at Lord's

Coronation Year and Titmus celebrates by hooking Surrey's Tony Lock for 6 at The Oval

He scored early centuries against Cambridge University and Hampshire to signal that he was in good form, but then injured a groin while bowling in Sid Brown's benefit match against Sussex at Lord's. Although he came back to score his third century of the season at Derby in July, Robertson's injury cost him his record of the only batsman to score 2,000 runs in every season since the war. In fact, Robertson failed even to make 1,000 runs in Championship games.

Of the other batsmen, Routledge finished third in the averages behind Edrich and Denis Compton, thanks to a score of 121 made by Worcester on his first Championship appearance of the season. Routledge played in ten games but, although considered an all-rounder with his medium-pacers, he bowled only six overs in the Championship and did not take a wicket.

After drawing with Surrey in early August, Middlesex lost their next three games, to Worcestershire and Gloucestershire at Lord's, and to Surrey at The Oval where the only redeeming feature was a sparkling innings by Denis Compton who hit 63 out of 77 added in 50 minutes with Edrich. Compton's characteristic knock

> **Denis Compton celebrated his 35th birthday on 23 May 1953 by scoring a brilliant unbeaten 143 against Sussex at Lord's. He hit seventeen 4s and his last 40 runs came in only 20 minutes.**

contained two 6s and six 4s and was made in spite of a brutish Oval track. The loss of three games in quick succession cost Middlesex any chance they might have had of a higher place. Yet how impossible failure seemed at Lord's in early July when Edrich scored 211 and Middlesex cruised to a big win over Essex.

Yet again, however, the Middlesex bowling was beyond reproach. Fred Titmus, the young off-spinner, took ninety-four wickets in the Championship matches alone and in all games he claimed 105 victims, turning the ball a great deal and developing the one that went away with the arm. Jack Young again headed the averages with 116 championship wickets at 19.05 each, and young Alan Moss took seventy-three in the Championship and earned himself a place on the MCC tour to the West Indies that winter. John Warr, the last amateur to give Middlesex such yeoman service, had forty-three victims and Don Bennett, who was only sixteen when he first played for Middlesex, took forty-one wickets and might have claimed many more but for the fact that he had to wait until Moss and Warr were through with the new ball. Bennett also scored useful runs and topped the 1,000 mark, averaging 29.91 to stake his claim as an all-rounder.

Middlesex had benefited by having Edrich as sole captain and there was a much more stable look to the handling of the side. In the match with the Australians at Lord's, rain ended play shortly after lunch on the first day. The match was thus doomed to a draw and Lindsey Hassett opted for batting practice before the Fourth Test at Leeds later that week. Middlesex made 150 and Australia replied with 416 all out, leaving the county 266 behind with 110 minutes to play. They lost Robertson, Sharp, Edrich and Brown in scoring 112 by the close of a tedious day.

FIRST CLASS RESULTS 1953
Championship Record

P	W	L	D	Tied	No Dcsn	Pos
28	10	5	11	1	1	5th

May
2-5   tied with Northants at Peterborough
6-8   lost to Cambridge University by three wickets at Fenners
9-12   beat Hampshire by eight wickets at Lord's
13-15   drew with Derbyshire at Lord's
16-19   drew with Essex at Westcliff
23-6   beat Sussex by 101 runs at Lord's
27-9   beat Oxford University by 15 runs at The Parks
May 30, **June** 1-2   no decision against Northants at Lord's

June
3-5   lost to Somerset by ten wickets at Lord's
6-9   drew with Yorkshire at Lord's
10-12   beat Leicestershire by innings and 56 runs at Lord's
13-16   beat Worcestershire by seven wickets at Worcester
17-19   beat Nottinghamshire by 20 runs at Lord's
20-3   lost to Gloucestershire by six wickets at Bristol

24-6   drew with Nottinghamshire at Trent Bridge
27-30   drew with Lancashire at Old Trafford
July
1-3   beat Essex by 141 runs at Lord's
4-7   beat Warwickshire by 148 runs at Edgbaston
11-14   drew with Yorkshire at Bradford
15-17   drew with Derbyshire at Derby
18-21   drew with the Australians at Lord's
22-3   beat Kent by ten wickets at Lord's
25-8   drew with Glamorgan at Cardiff
29-31   beat Hampshire by 82 runs at Southampton

August
1-4   drew with Sussex at Hove
5-7   beat Kent by 99 runs at Canterbury
8-11   drew with Surrey at Lord's
15-18   lost to Worcestershire by ten wickets at Lord's
19-21   lost to Gloucestershire by innings and 82 runs at Lord's
22-5   lost to Surrey by 135 runs at The Oval
August 29-31, **September** 1   drew with Lancashire at Lord's

1954

A Dismal Summer

Middlesex were making a habit of starting the season with a bang and then fizzling away like a damp squib. In 1954 they won their first six matches and then allowed the Championship to slip from them with some extremely indifferent performances in the closing weeks of the season. Denis Compton missed much of the season through a combination of representative calls, knee trouble and lumbago. Yet in the very first game, against Hampshire at Lord's, he scored a dazzling 117 in the first innings, 64 in the second, and captured eight Hampshire wickets in the match with figures of five for 19 and three for 58. In the second innings of the match Bill

Leslie Compton's benefit match against bottom-of-the-table Sussex at Lord's in June saw Middlesex lose their 100 per cent Championship record. Only rain, which washed out the third day, prevented a possible Sussex win and Middlesex were ultimately happy to settle for a draw. Collections for the beneficiary totalled over £700.

Edrich scored 105 before being stumped by Harrison off Shackleton and Middlesex triumphed by 135 runs when Hampshire collapsed a second time.

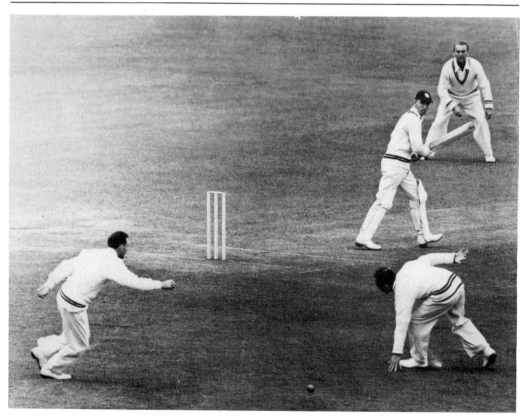

Robertson puts Notts' Arthur Jepson through the slips for 4

Against Worcester at Lord's in the second game, Compton and Edrich were again in superb form. In the first innings Edrich scored 141 with some powerful hooking; in the second Compton made 113 and was seen dancing down the wicket to the medium pace of Reg Perks. Perks took six for 76 but he could find no answer to a vintage Compton who played with all his old dash and aggression. Just for a time it seemed that his knee trouble did not exist. Worcester needed 281 to win but fell 30 runs short with Moss following up his

Once again the bowling showed more authority. In a summer when off-spinners thrived, twenty-one-year-old Freddie Titmus took 103 wickets in the Championship, and Bill Edrich managed to top the bowling averages with eight wickets at 17.62 runs each. Jack Young came in with ninety victims, John Warr with forty-three and Alan Moss with sixty-nine, despite breaking a bone in his foot, an injury which was not immediately obvious. Moss had finished second in the MCC West Indies tour averages in all

Fred Titmus, then 21, took 103 Championship wickets for Middlesex in 1954

haul of four wickets in the first innings with seven for 101 in the second.

At one stage, with Kenyon and Outschoorn putting 159 for the first wicket, a Middlesex victory looked highly unlikely until Moss, who bowled unchanged for almost three hours, broke through and ten Hampshire wickets fell for less than 100 runs. In a wet summer there were three Middlesex Championship games which did not get as far as deciding the issue of first innings and in the latter half of this dreadful summer the county batsmen suffered, none more so than Jack Robertson. Although Robertson scored 1,292 in all Championship innings, 557 of these came in just five innings, four of his five centuries being scored in the last two weeks of July. So, those runs apart, his consistency for the majority of the season was well below the form which had made him one of cricket's leading post-war run makers.

first-class games in 1953-4, although he played in only one Test. Denis Compton (twenty-five wickets) and Don Bennett (twenty-four) also gave valuable support in the Championship in 1954

Right in the middle of their dismal August, Middlesex scored a fine 96-run win over Yorkshire at Headingley. Norman Yardley put Middlesex in to bat and his decision seemed justified as the batsmen struggled to reach 197 with John Dewes top scorer with 45. When Yorkshire batted it was a similar story and apart from a dogged 52 from Brian Close, the White Rose county disintegrated before Young and Moss, and were dismissed for 113. When Middlesex batted a second time, Bob Appleyard followed up his six wickets in the first innings with four more and Middlesex were all out for 131, leaving Yorkshire to score 216 for victory. The rain-affected pitch gave them no chance and the spin of Young (four for 53) and Titmus (six for 50) took Middlesex to a wholly unexpected triumph.

Middlesex's last first-class match of 1954 saw them lose heavily to the Pakistani tourists. Pakistan batted first on a slow pitch and were able to declare at 303 for seven with Maqsood Ahmed scoring a stylish 76 before being stumped by Leslie Compton off the bowling of Jack Young. Only Don Bennett (59) and Fred Titmus (54 not out) put up any real fight and

Middlesex were dismissed for 175. When Pakistan batted again there were fine innings from Alim-ud-Din (85), Maqsood Ahmed again (63) and Imtiaz Ahmed (47 not out) which enabled them to declare a second time at 232 for five and set Middlesex 361 for victory. After an opening stand of 90 between Robertson and Brown, Middlesex folded and only young Titmus (61) again resisted. At 220 all out Middlesex went down by 140 runs.

FIRST CLASS RESULTS 1954
Championship Record

	P	W	L	D	No Dcsn	Pos
	28	10	5	10	3	7th =

May
8-11 beat Hampshire by 135 runs at Lord's
12-14 beat Worcestershire by 30 runs at Lord's
15-17 beat Nottinghamshire by seven wickets at Lord's
19-21 beat Somerset by one wicket at Lord's
22-5 beat Hampshire by three wickets at Southampton
26-8 drew with Oxford University at The Parks
May 29, **June** 1 beat Gloucestershire by seven wickets at Lord's

June
2-4 beat Cambridge University by four wickets at Fenners
5-8 drew with Sussex at Lord's
9-11 no decision in match with Lancashire at Old Trafford
12-15 beat Somerset by nine wickets at Bath
16-18 no decision in match with Glamorgan at Swansea
19-22 drew with Yorkshire at Lord's
23-5 beat Leicestershire by ten wickets at Lord's
26-9 lost to Kent by 42 runs at Lord's
June 30, **July** 1-2 drew with Warwickshire at Edgbaston

July
10-13 lost to Essex by innings and 67 runs at Chelmsford
14-16 drew with Leicestershire at Leicester
17-20 drew with Northants at Lord's
21-3 lost to Glamorgan by 22 runs at Lord's
24-7 drew with Northants at Northampton
28-30 beat Worcestershire by eight wickets at Worcester
July 31, **August** 2-3 lost to Sussex by eight wickets at Hove

August
4-6 drew with Kent at Canterbury
7-10 drew with Surrey at The Oval
11-13 drew with Warwickshire at Lord's
14-16 beat Yorkshire by 96 runs at Headingley
18-20 no decision in game with Derbyshire at Chesterfield
21-3 lost to Surrey by innings and 19 runs at Lord's
25-7 drew with Lancashire at Lord's
28-31 lost to the Pakistanis by 140 runs at Lord's

At Lord's on September 1-2, Middlesex lost to a Canadian touring team by three runs in a two day match which is not ranked first class.

1955

The Record Breaker

This time there was no 'Jeykell and Hyde' Middlesex like the fine starts and dismal finales of previous summers. In 1955 the county were an inconsistent side again, but this time the inconsistencies were dotted throughout the season. Again it was the same sorry story — a fine, all-round bowling attack which was not supported by the batsmen. Denis Compton again missed well over half the Championship season, playing only eleven of the twenty-eight games, and he scored only 590 runs at an average of 31.05, and that included one innings of 150 against Sussex at Lord's (Compton's only other century in 1955 was 158 in the Old Trafford Test against the South Africans). Bill Edrich, too, disappointed and he managed to average only 26.44, playing in all the Championship games but scoring only one century (125 not out at Edgbaston). His only other three-figure innings in 1955 came in a Gents v Players match at Scarborough.

On the other hand there was better news of Jack Robertson who recovered his form to the extent of scoring 1,754 for Middlesex in the Championship, nearly 500 more than the next-best player. The highlight of his season was 137 against Somerset at Lord's. The two men who gave most cause for pleasure on the batting front were, however, two amateurs, John Dewes and G. P. S. Delisle. Dewes, the former Cambridge Blue, scored 644 runs in seven matches to head the Middlesex averages with 53.66, and Delisle, who won his Oxford Blue in 1955, hit 636 in 13 games to average 25.44.

Both men scored centuries for Middlesex, Dewes scoring 117 against Sussex at Hove, and an unbeaten 101 against Surrey at The Oval, while Delisle made 105 at Trent Bridge, as well as scoring 113 for Oxford University against Gloucestershire at The Parks. For his feat against Nottinghamshire, Delisle received his Middlesex cap.

Robertson sweeps Smith of Essex to the Lord's boundary

But it was the bowling which took the Middlesex honours in 1955 and there was no one more outstanding than Freddie Titmus. Titmus took 137 wickets in the Championship and 158 in all matches for the county to beat A. E. Trott's record of 154 which had stood for well over half-a-century. And he became the first Middlesex player to do the double since R. W. V. Robins and N E. Haig in 1929. Titmus was selected to play in two Tests against South Africa and he was included in the MCC party for Pakistan to complete a fine season and herald his arrival as a fully-fledged world-class cricketer.

Titmus led the county averages and behind him came Alan Moss, Jack Young and John Warr. Although Bob Hurst, a left-arm spinner, squeezed into third place in the averages with eleven wickets, Titmus, Moss, Young and Warr were the men who collected 392 county scalps between them in 1955. Alan Moss took 100 wickets for Middlesex for the first time and he too was chosen to go to Pakistan.

Struggling Kent beat Middlesex twice and even bottom county Somerset managed to score a rare victory over them. But, as always, there were some moments of vintage Middlesex cricket. Denis Compton's brilliant 150 against Sussex, in the joint benefit match of Sharp and Thompson, lifted the gloom from a game which rain restricted to two days. Compton

Denis Compton missed well over half the Championship season

Fred Titmus took 158 wickets in all matches to pass Albert Trott's record and became the first Middlesex player to do the double since 1929

> **Against Somerset at Bath in June 1955 Fred Titmus took fifteen wickets for 95 runs in the match but still finished up on the losing side.**

dominated the Middlesex first innings, making his 150 out of 195 before he was caught on the boundary's edge by Suttle off the bowling of Marlar. A crowd of more than 20,000 gave him a standing ovation as he returned to the pavilion, for he certainly lit up their Whit Monday afternoon.

The other big Middlesex highlight of 1955 was a repeat victory over Yorkshire at Headingley in August. The previous season Middlesex had put paid to Yorkshire's chances of taking the Championship with a 96-run win. This time they achieved victory in a similarly emphatic manner. The Leeds wicket was damaged by rain and, after Middlesex put them in, Yorkshire struggled to make 151. It was little easier for Middlesex who managed 159, thanks to some resolute batting by Dewes, Edrich and Delisle as Freddie Trueman took four wickets for 52, and Cowan six for 52. When Yorkshire batted again, Titmus and Young spun them out for 175, leaving Middlesex to score 168 to win. There was an early shock when Trueman had Dewes caught behind with the score at nine, but fine batting by Robertson (82) and Brown (28) who added 67 for the second wicket saw Middlesex on the way to a five-wicket win. Don Bennett was there at the end with an unbeaten 24.

FIRST CLASS RESULTS 1955
Championship Record

P	W	L	D	Pos
28	14	12	2	5th

May

7-10 drew with Derbyshire at Lord's

11-13 beat Essex by 70 runs at Lord's

14-17 beat Hampshire by 55 runs at Lord's

18-20 drew with Oxford University at The Parks

21-4 beat Northants by six wickets at Rushden

25-7 lost to Gloucestershire by 60 runs at Bristol

28-31 drew with Sussex at Lord's

June

1-3 beat Cambridge University by three wickets at Fenners

4-6 beat Worcestershire by innings and 110 runs at Lord's

8-10 lost to Kent by six wickets at Lord's

11-13 lost to Lancashire by innings and 13 runs at Lord's

18-21 beat Somerset by nine wickets at Lord's

22-4 lost to Leicestershire by six wickets at Leicester

29-30 lost to Somerset by 63 runs at Bath

July

2-5 beat Worcestershire by eight wickets at Worcester

9-12 lost to Warwickshire by one wicket at Edgbaston

13-15 beat Lancashire by two wickets at Liverpool

16-19 lost to Yorkshire by eight wickets at Lord's

20-2 beat Northants by 13 runs at Lord's

23-6 lost to Hampshire by innings and six runs at Bournemouth

27-9 beat Glamorgan by one wicket at Cardiff

July 30, **August** 1-2 beat Sussex by six wickets at Hove

August

3-5 lost to Nottinghamshire by seven wickets at Trent Bridge

6-9 lost to Surrey by 39 runs at The Oval

10-11 beat Warwickshire by 24 runs at Lord's

13-16 beat Yorkshire by five wickets at Headingley

17-19 beat Glamorgan by 164 runs at Lord's

20-3 lost to Surrey by nine wickets at Lord's

24-6 beat Leicestershire by 40 runs at Lord's

27-30 lost to the South Africans by 235 runs at Lord's

August 31, **September** 1-2 lost to Kent by nine wickets at Folkestone

1956

Edrich Marches On

The wet summer of 1956 saw several new faces in the Middlesex side as players who had given the county stout service over the years moved over to make way for youth and potential. Among those who were no longer a part of the Middlesex senior side were Leslie Compton, Jack Young, Sid Brown, Alec Thompson and Harry Sharp. John Murray made immense strides as Leslie Compton's replacement behind the stumps and in his first full season he had 77 victims (63 caught and 14 stumped) in all matches, more than any wicketkeeper in the country. In additon, Murray was used as an opening batsman on many occasions and his top score was 48 against Gloucestershire at Lord's.

There were other notable young players coming through in 1956. Batsmen Peter Parfitt, Ron Hooker and Bob Gale all performed well while other players Angus (an opening bowler), Bick (batsman and occasional off-spinner), Baldry (a stylish batsman) and Hurst and Tilley (bowlers) played in a handful of matches and all gave flashes of potential. With the departure of so many old hands, and the blooding of quite a number of young players, Middlesex could be well satisfied with the eventual fifth place in the Championship, although two old faces at Lord's remained to play valuable batting roles.

At the age of forty Bill Edrich showed no sign of the advancing years. He topped the averages with 1,427 runs in the Championship at an average of 32.43 and his greatest innings of the summer was at Chesterfield where he became one of only eight players to score a double century in 1956. Derbyshire had won at Lord's but Middlesex had the best of the Chesterfield match where Edrich cut, chopped and hooked his way to a brilliant unbeaten 208 (four 6s and thirty-two 4s). Edrich added 139 for the fourth wicket with Baldry in 119 minutes, and 176 for the fifth wicket

Surrey's Micky Stewart pulls Titmus at The Oval but is caught on the boundary by Robertson for 25

with Hooker in only 95 minutes. Hooker was making his debut and after an uneasy start he settled down to score an unbeaten 77 as Middlesex powered to 408 for four declared and an eventual innings win.

Jack Robertson was the other batting mainstay of 1956. He scored 1,386 runs at 29.48 each and scored two centuries — 115 at Gloucester and 109 at Maidstone. Denis Compton, plagued by the knee injury which resulted in him having his right knee cap removed, played in only eight Championship games but, despite a limp, he made 110 at Glastonbury and 101 against Kent at Lord's, a revival which won him back his place against the Australians in the Fifth Test at The Oval where the old master scored 94 and 35 not out. The First Test at Trent Bridge had cost Middlesex dearly when Moss tore a stomach muscle and was out for much of the season. John Warr compensated Middlesex by having his best-ever season with 102 wickets at 16.42 each, Don Bennett took sixty-six, and while he was not as effective as his fine season of 1955, Fred Titmus still managed the double in all matches.

There were some staggeringly low totals in 1956, thanks to the awful summer which cricket once again endured. Middlesex were bowled out for less than 70 on four occassions, twice by Surrey, and once each by Hampshire and Kent. In contrast, Middlesex themselves dismissed Warwickshire for 55 at Lord's and Gloucestershire for 69 at Gloucester. In the Warwickshire match Middlesex won by ten wickets after Warr (six for 27) and Moss (four for 28) wrought havoc among the Midlanders' batting. At Gloucester it was Warr again (six for 33) and Bennett (four for 35) who did the damage. Robert-

son scored 115 as Middlesex replied with 330 for eight declared and although a fine 156 by Tom Graveney took Gloucestershire to 331 in their second innings, the damage had already been done and Middlesex coasted home by nine wickets.

Perhaps the best win — certainly the most satisfying — came at Lord's when

In his first full season John Murray had more victims than any other wicketkeeper in the county

Kent were beaten by an innings and 73 runs, thanks to some fine all-round performances. Denis Compton scored 101 in three hours and ten minutes to help Middlesex to 304 for five declared. Then Warr took five for 27 as Kent crumbled to 110 all out, and then followed up that with a career-best of nine for 65 in their second innings as they folded to 121. The other wicket was picked up by Titmus who had Pettiford stumped by Murray.

Middlesex had no answer to Kent's D. V. P. Wright at Maidstone in July when he took eight for 30 as Middlesex collapsed to 64 all out. Even a brave 109 by Robertson in the second innings could not save Middlesex from a nine-wicket defeat.

FIRST CLASS RESULTS 1956
Championship Record

P	W	L	D	No Dcsn	Pos
28	11	9	7	1	5th

May
2-4   drew with Oxford University at The Parks
9-11   drew with Nottinghamshire at Lord's
12-15   drew with Gloucestershire at Lord's
16-18   lost to Derbyshire by 88 runs at Lord's
19-21   lost to Sussex by innings and 22 runs at Lord's
23-5   beat Derbyshire by innings and 41 runs at Chesterfield
26-9   drew with Yorkshire at Sheffield
May 30-1, **June** 1   beat Cambridge University by five wickets at Fenners

June
2-5   beat Warwickshire by ten wickets at Lord's
6-8   no decision in the match with Worcestershire at Lord's
9-12   drew with Yorkshire at Lord's
13-14   lost to Lancashire by innings and 111 runs at Old Trafford
16-19   lost to Hampshire by nine wickets at Lord's
20-2   beat Nottinghamshire by seven wickets at Trent Bridge
23-6   beat Northants by seven wickets at Northampton

27-9   lost to Essex by 139 runs at Lord's
June 30, **July** 2-3   drew with Lancashire at Lord's

July
4-6   beat Essex by 115 runs at Westcliff
7-10   drew with Somerset at Glastonbury
14-17   beat Gloucestershire by nine wickets at Gloucester
18-20   lost to Kent by nine wickets at Maidstone
21-4   drew with the Australians at Lord's
25-7   beat Glamorgan by 77 runs at Lord's
28-31   beat Leicestershire by 84 runs at Loughborough

August
1-3   beat Hampshire by 12 runs at Southampton
4-7   beat Sussex by eight wickets at Hove
11-14   lost to Surrey by seven wickets at The Oval
15-17   beat Kent by innings and 73 runs at Lord's
18-21   lost to Surrey by 71 runs at Lord's
22-4   lost to Northants by two wickets at Lord's
25-8   drew with Worcestershire at Worcester

1957

Murray's Great Double

Middlesex once again gave a remarkable display of inconsistency in 1957 and of their first eleven Championship games they won five and lost six, their first drawn match not coming until the third week of June. The season was marked by the retirement from full-time cricket of Middlesex's 'twins', Denis Compton and Bill Edrich. Compton at last had to give in to the knee injury which had undergone three operations. Yet even in this last full season, when his footwork was affected, he still found the ability to score three centuries in the Championship with 143 against Worcestershire at Lord's, 109 at Leyton, and 104 at Old Trafford, to top the averages with 1,404 Championship runs at 37.94.

Bill Edrich, too, reached 1,000 runs but failed to score a century, his top Championship score being 77, while Jack Robertson, at the age of forty, returned to his best scoring 2,000 runs for the ninth time, with three centuries. His innings against Essex at Lord's in July was undoubtedly one of his greatest when he reached a double hundred for the last time in his career. Robertson scored an unbeaten 201 (twenty-eight 4s) as Middlesex were able to declare at 337 for six and ultimately beat Essex by a massive 209 runs after Titmus and Moss ran through them in the second innings when they were all out for 83. The conditions of another wet summer favoured the seam bowlers and with two months of the season gone, Titmus had claimed only thirty-eight victims, although he went on to do the double for the third successive season.

The wickets at Lord's favoured definite results and Middlesex saw only two games there reach stalemate — the tour game against the West Indians, and the Championship match against Leicestershire when not a ball was bowled due to rain. Alan Moss topped the Championship averages with ninety-four wickets and left-arm spinner Bob Hurst came second with seventy-two victims. Titmus had eighty-eight, John Warr thirty-five, Don Bennett, forty-one, and the old warhorse Compton winkled out thirty-five with his unorthodox left-arm spin. John Murray continued his magnificent work behind the stumps by becoming only the second wicketkeeper in history to score 1,000 runs and dismiss over 100 batsmen in one season.

The darkest day of the season so far as Middlesex were concerned came in July when they dismissed Derbyshire for a meagre 153 at Chesterfield, and yet still contrived to lose by an innings with the season's lowest score. Donald Carr put Middlesex in to bat and that fine seam bowler, Cliff Gladwin, took six for 23 as the visitors were bowled out for 102, with only Robertson (38) and Titmus (22) putting up much of a fight. When Derbyshire batted, Hurst and Tilly took four wickets each and only a seventh-wicket stand of 50 between George Dawkes and

Murray attemps to sweep Bruce Dooland (Notts) to leg at Lord's

Derek Morgan helped them to a respectable lead. When Middlesex batted again there was total disaster. The first nine wickets fell for only 13 runs and only lusty hitting by Don Bennett raised Middlesex to an embarrassing 29 all out with Bennett on an undefeated 14 runs. Gladwin took five for 18, Les Jackson three for 7, and Morgan weighed in with the last man, Moss. The damp pitch was to blame and Derbyshire adapted better than Middlesex.

Although the match against the West Indians was drawn, it was a most exciting affair and Middlesex only just failed to score what would have been an exceedingly fine win. Middlesex batted first and scored 144, the West Indians replied with 176, and Middlesex's second innings realised 213, leaving the tourists to score 182 at 66 an hour. Two wickets were down with only ten runs on the board and even a fine 61 by Frank Worrall still found the West Indians at 108 for six. Wes Hall hit

A fine catch by Murray dismisses Surrey's Clark off the bowling of Moss at The Oval

Middlesex had a taste of sweeter medicine at Dover in August when Titmus and Murray added 82 for their seventh wicket to haul them to an eventual 203 all out. Then Titmus and Moss dismissed Kent for 108, only to find themselves struggling at 86 for six before Titmus again came to the rescue with a heroic 70 (two 6s and nine 4s) and Middlesex were all out for 179. The Kent innings lasted only 75 minutes. Alan Moss returned the best figures of his career with seven for 24 (twelve for 59 in the match) and Kent were all out for 43, to leave Middlesex the victors by 231 runs.

At the end of 1957 Bill Edrich retired from full-time cricket and so ended five years as Middlesex skipper, a position he had shared with Denis Compton in 1951 and 1952.

Compton for 6, 6, 1, 4, 4, before being stumped, and with ten minutes to go, Ramadhin was bowled by Hurst with the score at 133. But Alexander and Dewdney held out for a draw and took the tourists to 143 for eight at the close.

FIRST CLASS RESULTS 1957
Championship Record

P	W	L	D	No Dcsn	Pos
28	10	12	3	3	7th

May

4-7   beat Nottinghamshire by 115 runs at Lord's

8-10   lost to Kent by innings and 59 runs at Lord's

11-14   beat Gloucestershire by 135 runs at Lord's

18-21   lost to Hampshire by 3 runs at Portsmouth

22-4   lost to Oxford University by four wickets at The Parks

25-8   beat Somerset by 9 runs at Lord's

29-31   beat Cambridge University by nine wickets at Fenners

June

1-4   lost to Northants by 47 runs at Lord's

5-7   lost to Derbyshire by 163 runs at Lord's

8-11   beat Sussex by 54 runs at Lord's

12-14   beat Hampshire by 116 runs at Lord's

15-18   lost to Yorkshire by ten wickets at Lord's

19-21   lost to Nottinghamshire by two wickets at Trent Bridge

22-5   drew with Yorkshire at Headingley

June 29, **July** 1-2 lost to Lancashire by 72 runs at Lord's

July

6-8   beat Worcestershire by 134 runs at Worcester

10-12   drew with Gloucestershire at Gloucester

13-16   no decision in match with Lancashire at Old Trafford

17-19   lost to Derbyshire by innings and 22 runs at Chesterfield

20-3   drew with the West Indians at Lord's

24-6   beat Essex by 209 runs at Lord's

27-30   beat Warwickshire by 47 runs at Edgbaston

July 31, **August** 1-2 lost to Essex by 74 runs at Leyton

August

3-6   lost to Sussex by 99 runs at Hove

7-9   drew with Northants at Northampton

10-13   no decision in match with Surrey at The Oval

14-16   no decision in match with Leicestershire at Lord's

17-20   lost to Surrey by 102 runs at Lord's

21-2   beat Kent by 231 runs at Dover

24-6   beat Glamorgan by seven wickets at Swansea

28-30   lost to Worcestershire by two wickets at Lord's

1958

Warr Leader

A feature of Middlesex Championship cricket in previous seasons had been that the side nearly always achieved a result, win or draw, and this positive play resulted in points and a healthy place in the table, although never a title in the 1950s. In 1958 all that changed and Middlesex drew no less than sixteen Championship games. Although it was another wet summer, the weather was not totally to blame for this string of indecisive results and one reason was a batting line-up which had lost key men, and which was still awaiting the maturity of the newly-introduced players. Middlesex started well enough, however, and until mid-June they were always in the first two. But after that they dropped away badly and after losing their unbeaten record to Kent by an innings at Lord's, the rest of their summer was one of indifferent displays. They lost three of their last seven games

and finished tenth.

With Bill Edrich retired from full-time cricket, John Warr took over as skipper of Middlesex and he handled the side well, especially considering that it was in a transitional stage. Warr also gave Alan Moss good support with the new ball and took sixty-seven wickets at 17.80 each to finish second in the Championship averages. Moss began the season in devastating form and he finished with 106 victims in the Championship at 16.95 apiece, and 126 at 16.82 in all games. Titmus had a lean start but after taking six for 86 against the New Zealanders his bowling season took off and he finished with seventy-one Championship wickets and eighty-seven in all matches. The most encouraging performance was that of Tilly who, given more opportunity in 1958, took forty-six Championship wickets.

Bill Edrich bowled by White of Hampshire for a single at Lord's

> **Middlesex were dismissed for 94 on a soft Lord's pitch in July when Higgs and Tattersall exploited the conditions to the full. Middlesex recovered well in their second knock, reaching 384 for seven declared to set Lancashire 291 in four hours. Warr and Bennett sent back the opening pair without a run scored but Pullar and Marner took Lancashire to 67 for two before the rain halted play and the match was drawn.**

Edrich played in thirteen Championship games, Compton in just three, but neither achieved anything of note, and it was Jack Robertson who was again the mainstay of the Middlesex batting. Although he failed to score a century (his highest innings was 99 against Sussex at Lord's in May when he was caught by Oakman off Marlar when trying a big hit in the direction of mid-on) Robertson easily topped the Championship averages with 1,467 runs at 34.92. Robertson was later dropped down the order to make way for Eric Russell and his presence in the middle order gave it some stability. Peter Parfitt, the stylish left-hander, made useful runs when on leave from the RAF and he finished second in the averages with 494 runs from twenty innings at 29.05 each. Parfitt, too, saw the tantilising 99 as his top score and Bob Gale was the only man to hit a century in the 1958 Championship for Middlesex.

Left-hander Gale made two three-figure scores —122 at Dover and 101 against Hampshire at Lord's — and he also scored a century for MCC against Oxford University at Lord's, but his overall consistency was not so good and his bigger innings were interspersed with many lean times. Nevertheless, Gale notched 1,333 Championship runs. Eric Russell began his opening partnership with Gale with great distinction at Leicester where the two put on 96 and 113 for the first wicket in a match which Middlesex might ultimately have lost. Declarations kept the game alive and Leicestershire needed six runs to win when stumps were drawn, although there was some confusion when the pavilion clock stopped! Murray and Titmus did little with the bat but Murray held seventy-four catches and claimed

four stumpings to finish leading wicket-keeper for the third year in a row.

The last win of Middlesex's bright start came at Lord's in early June when Hampshire went down by 70 runs. Middlesex were put into bat on a drying pitch and it was the tail-end batsmen who saw them to 149, with Warr leading a late recovery after eight wickets had fallen for 89 runs. Warr hit 30 before Derek Shackleton bowled him. The Hampshire seamer finished with six for 61. When Hampshire batted it was Moss's turn to revel in the conditions and he took seven for 68. Only a breezy stand of 64 in three-quarters of

Russell gets the ball past Peter May at The Oval

an hour between Colin Ingleby-Mackenzie and Barnard helped Hampshire to a first-innings lead of 21. Bob Gale's 101 (four 6s and ten 4s) and Peter Parfitt's 58, coupled with an unbeaten 52 from John Murray, enabled Middlesex to declare at 298 for nine, leaving Hampshire to get 277 in five hours and ten minutes. Gale and Parfitt had added 113 for the fourth wicket in under two hours. Hampshire again began badly to Moss and, although Ingleby-Mackenzie and Barnard again shared in a big stand (108), Titmus mopped up the later order and Middlesex were home.

After that, Middlesex's Championship successes were few and there was the bitter blow of losing to Kent by an innings. At Lord's Middlesex were put out for 87 after some splendid fast-medium bowling by David Haltyard who took six for 43; at Dover, the roles were reversed and after

Gale's second century of the season in the Championship, Titmus, Tilly and Moss bowled out Kent twice for 149 and 140 to win by an innings and 22 runs. The game against the New Zealanders saw the tourists robbed of certain victory by the weather. Needing only 125 in three hours and five minutes, Miller and Sutcliffe had time to take the score to three without loss when a downpour ended their hopes. In Middlesex's second innings Hooker (throat infection) and Moss (sprained wrist) were unable to bat.

FIRST CLASS RESULTS 1958
Championship Record

P	W	L	D	No Dcsn	Pos
28	7	4	16	1	10th

May

7-9 beat Nottinghamshire by two wickets at Lord's

10-13 beat Leicestershire by eight wickets at Lord's

17-20 drew with Worcestershire at Worcester

21-3 drew with Northamptonshire at Northampton

24-7 beat Sussex by eight wickets at Lord's

28-30 drew with Cambridge University at Fenners

June

4-6 beat Hampshire by 70 runs at Lord's

7-10 drew with Lancashire at Old Trafford

11-13 beat Oxford University by one wicket at The Parks

14-17 drew with Gloucestershire at Lord's

21-4 drew with Glamorgan at Cardiff

25-6 lost to Kent by innings and 26 runs at Lord's

July

2-4 drew with Warwickshire at Edgbaston

5-8 beat Somerset by eight wickets at Bath

12-15 drew with Yorkshire at Sheffield

16-18 drew with Leicestershire at Leicester

19-22 drew with the New Zealanders at Lord's

23-5 drew with Lancashire at Lord's

26-9 beat Glamorgan by six wickets at Lord's

July 30-31, **August** 1 drew with Derbyshire at Chesterfield

August

2-5 drew with Sussex at Hove

6-8 drew with Hampshire at Portsmouth

9-11 lost to Surrey by seven wickets at The Oval

13-15 drew with Worcestershire at Lord's

16-19 lost to Surrey by six wickets at Lord's

20-2 beat Kent by innings and 22 runs at Dover

23-6 drew with Essex at Southend

27-9 no decision in match with Northants at Lord's

August 30, **September** 1-2 lost to Warwickshire by 216 runs at Lord's

1959

Middlesex Miss Out

After the miserable summers of the previous few years, the 1959 season was tailor-made for cricket. The sun seemed to shine down endlessly, wickets were hard and true and runs fairly sizzled from the bat with Warwickshire's Mike Smith leading the way with 3,245. Yet for Middlesex the runs still seemed at a premium and the county did not share in the run glut of this most glorious of summers. They passed the 300-mark only rarely, and yet they did win the £500 prize for the fastest 200 in the first innings in 1959. That came at Trent Bridge in August when they scored their first 200 in 217 balls and ultimately declared at 397 for nine and won by 74 runs with Fred Titmus taking seven for 64 in Nottinghamshire's second innings.

But that match apart, Middlesex never found runs really easy to come by. New man Ted Clark topped the Championship averages with 728 runs at 34.66 and five players — Russell, Gale, Hooker, Titmus and Parfitt — passed the 1,000 mark. Clark showed splendid temperament in his first season and on his first-class

debut against Cambridge University he scored a century. His undefeated 100 came in exactly two hours. Clark was never afraid to play his shots and he emerged in 1959 as a fine striker of the ball. But the decline of Jack Robertson was sad. He was granted a second benefit this season but played in only thirteen games and scored 326 runs at a meagre average of 14.81.

Bob White played in sixteen Championship games and scored 605 runs with a top score of 54 not out in that run chase at Trent Bridge where, coincidently, he went to play and made more of a name for himself as an off-spinner than a batsman. Eric Russell began the season in great form, scoring six innings of over 50 in his first eight innings, but he did not maintain that consistency; and Bob Gale, scorer of most Championship runs with 1,503, also lacked the ability to score consistently big totals.

Fred Titmus did the double in Championship games alone with 1,242 runs and 102 wickets and he bowled a lot of overs —

Middlesex against Hampshire in the unusual setting of Hornsey when Lord's was unavailable

Middlesex's match with the Indians in 1959 was marked by the debut for the tourists of A. A. Baig, the Oxford University batsman who scored 102 in two hours. Middlesex had no answer to Borde's leg breaks in their second innings and left the tourists to score 67 to win. The Indians lost six wickets in reaching that total, thanks mainly to some carefree batting, and Bick picked up four cheap and unexpected wickets.

Ted Clark drops Indian Test batsman Polly Umrigar off Hooker's bowling during the match against the tourists at Lord's

more than 1,000. But Middlesex's attack was weakened by the loss of Alan Moss for ten games because of Test calls and injury. He took seventy-three Championship wickets and finished second in the averages behind his skipper, John Warr, whose 107 victims cost him 16.21 each. It was Titmus, Warr and Moss who bore the brunt of the attack. Hooker, Tilly, Hurst, Bick, Bennett and Gale all chipped in with valuable wickets, but Middlesex lacked the one bowler to compare with Titmus, Warr and Moss. Such a fourth bowler would have given to the side so much more

penetration, particularly with Moss missing for a quarter of the games, and would have transformed Middlesex into a much more effective side. John Murray took seventy-nine catches and made nine stumpings in all first-class matches to maintain his claim as one of England's leading wicketkeepers.

Twice in the first three Championship games of the season Middlesex won in nail-biting circumstances. Against Kent at Lord's they were all out for 203 in four hours and twenty minutes. The highlight of the Middlesex second knock had been a brisk 33 by John Warr who hit one 6 and six 4s off nine balls. When Kent batted a second time, a second-wicket stand of 149 between Cowdrey and Phebey gave them a grand start. Cowdrey hit three 6s and eight 4s, and Phebey twelve 4s. But the wickets tumbled as regularly as the runs came, and when last man Page strode to the wicket Kent still needed 20 in fifteen minutes. Eight minutes later Page and Brown had whittled that down to three runs and then Brown dragged a ball from Titmus on his stumps and Middlesex won by two runs.

In the very next game, against Surrey also at Lord's, Eric Russell was awarded his county cap with a sound performance of 52 and 32, Middlesex totalled 220 batting first; Sussex were dismissed for 130 with Titmus taking seven wickets; Middlesex's second innings amounted to 138, thanks largely to Parfitt's dogged 60; and then Sussex batted again, chasing 229 in reasonable time. Les Lenham was unable to open the Sussex innings because of an ankle injury and D. V. Smith deputised admirably, scoring 90 and putting on 102 for the third wicket with Ted Dexter (who was also awarded his cap in this match). At one stage Sussex were coasting at 208 for four when Moss and Warr struck and they were all out for 227 to give Middlesex victory by a single run. Moss finished with five for 42.

FIRST CLASS RESULTS 1959
Championship Record

P	W	L	D	Pos
28	10	9	9	10th

May

6-8   beat Warwickshire by 89 runs at Lord's

9-12   beat Kent by 2 runs at Lord's

16-19   beat Sussex by 1 run at Lord's

20-2   drew with Oxford University at The Parks

23-6   beat Kent by 109 runs at Gravesend

27-9   lost to Essex by innings and 22 runs at Lord's

May 30, **June** 1-2 lost to Derbyshire by six wickets at Lord's

June

3-5   beat Cambridge University by 233 runs at Fenners

6-9   beat Leicestershire by innings and 73 runs at Lord's

10-12   drew with Worcestershire at Lord's

13-16   drew with Somerset at Bath

17-19   drew with Lancashire at Liverpool

20-3   lost to Warwickshire by six wickets at Edgbaston

24-6   drew with Northamptonshire at Northampton

27-30   beat Somerset by innings and 119 runs at Lord's

July

4-6   lost to Glamorgan by 2 runs at Swansea

8-10   lost to Hampshire by two wickets at Hornsey

11-14   lost to Leicestershire by eight wickets at Ashby-de-la-Zouch

18-21   lost to the Indians by four wickets at Lord's

22-4   beat Lancashire by four wickets at Lord's

25-8   drew with Worcestershire at Worcester

29-31   beat Hampshire by 201 runs at Portsmouth

August

1-4   beat Sussex by nine wickets at Hove

5-7   lost to Yorkshire by four wickets at Scarborough

8-11   drew with Surrey at Lord's

12-14   lost to Gloucestershire by innings and 60 runs at Cheltenham

15-18   lost to Yorkshire by six wickets at Lord's

22-5   beat Nottinghamshire by 74 runs at Trent Bridge

26-8   drew with Northamptonshire at Lord's

August 29-30, **September** 1 drew with Surrey at The Oval

September

2-4   drew with Glamorgan at Lord's

1960

Moss the Magnificent

John Warr marked his last season as Middlesex captain by steering the side to third place in the Championship, their highest since they shared the title with Yorkshire in 1949. Indeed, had it not been for a poor spell towards the end of July and in early August, when three games were lost and several drawn, then Middlesex could well have come right back to take the county title outright for the first time since 1947.

Playing their early matches at Lord's, Middlesex took full advantage of home soil and for a short spell in mid-May they topped the table. In the very first county match of the season, they skittled Hampshire out for 82 at Lord's — Moss, Titmus and Bennett sharing the wickets — and finally won a breath-taking match by just one wicket. There were eight runs needed when last man Moss joined Murray and Hampshire really should have won when Roy Marshall missed Moss in the slips before Middlesex's wicketkeeper clipped the winning runs off Shackleton and the side were home at a perilous 82 for nine.

Other sides, too, found the full force of the Middlesex attack. Glamorgan were bowled out for 85 at Lord's (Moss five for 31), Yorkshire for 102 (Moss four for 32) and Glamorgan for 96 and 93 at Neath (where Moss finished with a match analysis of 13 for 51). Alan Moss had a superb season, taking 114 wickets for 12.50 each.

Although Alan Moss's opportunities for Test cricket were limited in 1960, he finished top of the England bowling averages with nine wickets for 15.33 runs apiece from 50.1 overs (seven maidens).

Moss was unlucky to play in only two Test Matches against the South Africans in 1960, and it was only the fine form of Trueman and Statham which kept the Middlesex paceman's chances down to a minimum. Moss could only hope to play when England needed a third seamer and the fact that he finished third in the national averages, behind Statham and Les Jackson, bears witness to his tremendous performances throughout the season. John Warr and Fred Titmus gave him immense support throughout 1960 and Titmus took ninety-nine wickets for the county and 117 in all first-class matches to bring him the double for the fifth time in six seasons.

Two batsmen with the same surname, but who were not related, gave Middlesex's line-up a stronger look during a season when their batting was always useful, but never outstanding. Eric Russell maintained his improvement and headed the averages with 1,604 runs at 35.64 per innings, while newcomer Sid Russell, born at Feltham, weighed in with 1,002 runs at 31.31. The two men could not have

been further apart in style, despite their similarity of name. While Eric, a Scotsman was an elegant player with a fine repertoire of off-side strokes and delicate leg-glances, Sid was a rumbustuous and somewhat unorthodox batsman with a lusty square-cut as his main weapon.

Bob Gale finished second in the batting averages with 1,079 runs at 34.80 runs per innings and although he missed several games through injury, Gale showed a tremendous amount of ability in the nineteen games in which he did play. Peter Parfitt, scorer of two centuries in 1960, was a young player who augered well for the future, and with Eric Russell playing himself into the Players side against the Gentlemen, as well as winning a place on the MCC tour to New Zealand, Middlesex cricket looked in a healthy state.

The highlights of 1960 were undoubtedly the two victories over Surrey, who Middlesex had not beaten since 1948. At The Oval, Middlesex won the toss and made 284 for 7 declared before bowling out Surrey for 71 and 192, with Titmus taking five for 24 in the first innings, to win by an innings and 21 runs. When the sides met at Lord's later in the month, Middlesex won by eight wickets with Gale and Sid Russell seeing them through with about twenty minutes to spare. This match was the last appearance at Lord's as a professional cricketer of Alec Bedser.

In the final game of 1960 Middlesex failed to take any points and missed the runners-up spot. Doug Slade of Worcestershire spun them out for 143 on a soft pitch at Lord's. Worcestershire replied with 235 for eight declared, although no play was possible on the second day, and when Middlesex batted again they slumped to 62 for eight before Moss and Drybrough played out time.

South Africa's Tom Goddard drives Bick to the boundary at Lord's

FIRST CLASS RESULTS 1960
Championship Record

P	W	L	D	Pos
28	12	4	12	3rd

May
4-6   beat Cambridge University by 113 runs at Fenners
7-10   beat Hampshire by one wicket at Lord's
11-13   drew with Derbyshire at Burton
14-17   beat Glamorgan by 254 runs at Lord's
21-4   beat Oxford University by 139 runs at The Parks
25-7   beat Notts by nine wickets at Lord's
28-31   beat Somerset by nine wickets at Lord's

June
1-3   beat Leicestershire by ten wickets at Lord's
4-7   drew with Sussex at Lord's
11-14   drew with Yorkshire at Lord's
15-16   beat Glamorgan by five wickets at Neath
18-21   drew with Lancashire at Old Trafford
22-4   drew with Yorkshire at Headingley
25-8   lost to Warwickshire by 38 runs at Edgbaston

July
2-4   drew with Somerset at Glastonbury
6-8   drew with Essex at Westcliff
9-12   drew with Kent at Lord's
16-19   drew with the South Africans at Lord's
20-2   drew with Essex at Lord's
23-6   beat Kent by 110 runs at Blackheath
27-9   beat Northants by innings and 14 runs at Kettering

July 31, **August** 1-2 lost to Sussex by 202 runs at Hove

August
3-5   lost to Hampshire by innings and 26 runs at Portsmouth
6-9   beat Surrey by innings and 21 runs at The Oval
10-12   lost to Gloucestershire by 29 runs at Lord's
13-16   beat Surrey by eight wickets at Lord's
17-19   drew with Gloucestershire at Cheltenham
20-3   beat Worcestershire by ten wickets at Worcester
24-6   drew with Warwickshire at Lord's
27-30   beat Lancashire by 132 runs at Lord's

August 31, **September** 1-2 drew with Worcestershire at Lord's

1961
Many a Slip

With John Warr retired from first-class cricket, Ian Bedford was tempted back to Lord's to take charge of the side in 1961. His first season as captain started in disastrous fashion when Middlesex lost to Northants and Essex in the opening matches. In the first game Northants triumphed by three wickets with only ten minutes of the match remaining when Subba Row, who was injured and batted at number nine in the second innings, hit the winning run with a classic off-drive off the bowling of Moss. At Brentwood in the next match Essex batted first and made 326 on an easy pitch, although Titmus finished with the respectable figures of five for 62. Middlesex made 172 in their first innings when Knight, Bailey and Preston took three wickets each, and an unbeaten 62 by Savill enabled Essex to declare at 187 for seven, leaving Middlesex 342 for victory. They never looked like getting them. There were useful runs from several batsmen, but no one came up with the major innings which Middlesex needed, and Essex won by 115 runs.

It was a bad start and yet by the third week of July, Middlesex were top of the table. They won twelve out of their next fifteen matches after Brentwood, drew the other three, and with 156 points out of a possible 210, went from bottom to top. Alas, they lost four games out of the next seven and even a rousing finish, with Yorkshire and Gloucestershire beaten in the last two matches, could not give

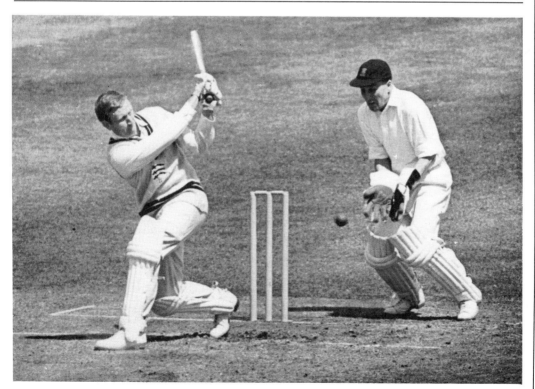

Sid Russell attempts a big hit off Paddy Phelan of Essex during the game at Lord's

Middlesex the Championship. They finished third, but it was a splendid effort and, but for a couple of slips, they may have topped the table.

Ironically, Bedford missed the first match of the Middlesex revival when he was injured and could not play against Essex at Lord's, Alan Moss taking over the side. It was Moss who set up the victory with five for 57 as Essex made 236, with Doug Insole run out for 60. Middlesex's reply was 262 and Sid Russell top-scorer with 73. Indeed, Sid Russell was the only batsman who looked comfortable, once openers Eric Russell and Bob Gale had departed after an opening stand of 79. When Essex batted again, Moss was again among the wickets with the scalps of Bear, Knight and Greensmith. But it was Don Bennett, Middlesex's sturdy Yorkshireman from Wakefield, who broke the back of the Essex innings, removing Baker, Smith, Insole and Bailey for a personal cost of 46 runs. Middlesex needed 221 in three and a half hours. Eric Russell batted splendidly for 91, putting on 94 with Gale for the first wicket, and Parfitt and Sid Russell took Middlesex close before Sid Russell was caught by Taylor off Knight. White was held by Bailey off the same bowler, and then Parfitt (44 not out) and Titmus squeezed Middlesex through with three minutes to spare.

> One of the finest innings seen at Lord's in 1961 was Australian Ken Mackay's 168 against Middlesex for the tourists. MacKay scored 92 before lunch on the first day. He hit one 6 and twenty-seven 4s — and was dropped when he had scored only 12!

Middlesex won their next game, again with little time to spare. Eric Russell scored a magnificent 156 against Sussex at Lord's. When Middlesex batted again they had been set 231 in two hours and fifty-five minutes. Gale made 81 and Eric Russell 45, the pair opening with a stand of 80, and when Middlesex's third wicket fell they still needed 64 runs in less than three quarters of an hour. It was left to Parfitt, once again, to get them, with Murray chipping in with an unbeaten 20. Parfitt's contribution was 52 not out and Middlesex took twelve points from the game with just nine minutes to spare. And

Mickey Stewart bowled by Don Bennett for 11 at The Oval

so the charge went on, right through until halfway through July when Middlesex fell short of the required momentum.

Certainly, the Middlesex batting was showing immense promise in 1961, Eric Russell, Parfitt, Gale and Titmus each scored over 1,500 runs and Clark also reached the 1,000-mark. Parfitt topped the averages with 1,814 Championship runs at 37.79, and he made over 2,000 in all games to earn himself a place on that winter's tour to India and Pakistan. Fred Titmus did the double yet again, achieving the feat in Championship games alone, and John Murray's continued fine form won him a Test place against the Australians. Murray played in all five Tests and in all first-class matches he claimed ninety-three victims, just one short of Yorkshire's Jimmy Binks.

But the bowling presented some problems and John Warr was sorely missed.

Moss and Titmus again headed the averages (Moss had 112 Championship wickets at 18.56; Titmus 123 at 21.58) and Hooker came on with sixty-seven wickets in the Championship now that he was used more as a bowler. Bennett also played well enough to claim sixty-seven wickets, but Middlesex lacked another truly front-line bowler. Middlesex's other great need was a spinner to support Titmus and although the left-armers Bob Hurst and Colin Drybrough played in some great games, neither was the answer. In truth, skipper Bedford could have made more use of his own leg-break and googly bowling but he restricted himself to 303 overs, claiming thirty-two wickets at 29.43. In 1961 a young amateur named J. M. Brearley from Cambridge University played in two games and scored 42 runs in four innings.

FIRST CLASS RESULTS 1961
Championship Record

P	W	L	D	No Dcsn	Pos
28	15	6	6	1	3rd

May

6-9	lost to Northants by three wickets at Lord's
10-12	lost to Essex by 115 runs at Brentwood
13-16	drew with Oxford University at The Parks
17-19	beat Essex by six wickets at Lord's
20-3	beat Sussex by seven wickets at Lord's
27-30	beat Somerset by six wickets at Taunton

May 31, **June** 1-2 drew with Lancashire at Lord's

June

3-6	beat Warwickshire by five wickets at Lord's
7-9	drew with Kent at Lord's
10-13	beat Somerset by two wickets at Lord's
14-16	beat Yorkshire by 175 runs at Bradford
17-20	beat Warwickshire by six wickets at Edgbaston
24-7	beat Nottinghamshire by 28 runs at Trent Bridge
28-30	beat Hampshire by 131 runs at Lord's

July

1-4	beat Glamorgan by nine wickets at Lord's
8-11	beat Gloucestershire by one wicket at Gloucester
12-14	no decision in match with Lancashire at Old Trafford
15-18	beat Surrey by 61 runs at The Oval
19-21	lost to Kent by 30 runs at Maidstone
22-5	lost to the Australians by ten wickets at Lord's
26-8	lost to Derbyshire by seven wickets at Lord's
29-31	drew with Hampshire at Portsmouth

August

2-4	beat Leicestershire by 28 runs at Leicester
5-8	drew with Sussex at Hove
9-11	lost to Worcestershire by 15 runs at Worcester
12-15	lost to Surrey by 29 runs at Lord's
16-18	drew with Glamorgan at Llanelly
23-5	drew with Worcestershire at Lord's
26-9	beat Yorkshire by 85 runs at Lord's

September

2-5	beat Gloucestershire by 152 runs at Lords

1962

Parfitt's Season

The absence of another bowler of the highest class to support Moss and Titmus was never more apparent than in 1962 when, although they lost eight games, only two more than the previous summer, Middlesex slipped from third place down to thirteenth — the county's lowest since 1950. Alan Moss suffered most from the strain imposed by having to carry the new-ball attack almost single handed; and to compound the problem Ian Bedford was injured and played in only half the matches, which meant that Moss was called upon to lead the side in addition to carrying the responsibility of breaking down the opposition's early order. Hooker and Bennett were never in a position to offer Moss the support he needed and neither did as well as in 1961. The only real bowling success was Fred Titmus who took 110 Championship wickets at exactly 20 runs each. Colin Drybrough did well when he came into the side after the Oxford University season, taking thirty-eight wickets at 28.36, but he never had the class of the first-rate spinner which Middlesex needed.

The batting was becoming more settled, however, and Parfitt topped the Middlesex Championship averages with 1,308 at 39.63 (discounting Pearman's 244 runs at 40.66, for he played only six complete innings). Parfitt scored 2,121 runs in all first-class matches to finish ninth in the English averages with 45.12 and he hit eight centuries. Two of them came in Middlesex's match with the Pakistanis, and three more in the Tests at Headingley, Edgbaston and Trent Bridge. His highest innings of 1962 was 138 against Essex at Lord's in May.

Parfitt certainly relished the Pakistani

John Edrich is well caught by Roger Pearman on the last day of the match at The Oval. Don Bennett is the bowler

bowling in 1962 and his Test average was 113.33. Other Middlesex batsmen were in equally good form in the Championship. Bob Gale scored 1,793 runs (and over 2,000 in all games) and he hit four centuries during the season, including one innings of 200 against Glamorgan at Newport where he batted for five hours and struck one 6 and twenty-four 4s, sharing century partnerships with Eric Russell and Ted Clarke. Don Bennett also had a fine match, taking five for 61 in Glamorgan's first innings. The individual performances were not enough to win the game, however, and Glamorgan batted out time comfortably on the third day. Eric Russell, Bob Hooker and Bob White all did well with the bat and Titmus and Clarke gave good support. John Murray was unfit for the early part of the season and he failed to contribute with the bat, though he did win back his place for the last three Tests.

One young player who came into the Middlesex side in 1962 was Mike Smith, born at Enfield and signed as an all-rounder who bowled left-arm slows and who was a useful batsman. In his first season Smith made 650 runs in twenty-eight innings and averaged 27.08, as well as taking fourteen wickets at a cost of 43.50. It would be some time before Smith won a permanent place in the side but when he did, it signalled the start of another famous Middlesex opening partnership when he teamed up with Eric Russell.

Middlesex's form over the previous seasons had given hope that they might challenge for the title in 1962, but the lack of bowling penetration cost them dearly and although, as we have seen, they lost only two more games than in 1961, they found it hard to win matches. No less than thirteen Championship games were drawn and this reflected the fact that Middlesex could not bowl out opponents cheaply enough to give themselves a scent of victory. The early Lord's fixtures, for so often the launching pad for a sustained attack on the Championship, brought a mixed bag of fortune and only the six-wicket win over Yorkshire in early June gave hope for the immediate future. Yorkshire declared their first innings closed at 297 for nine before a fine 133 from Gale enabled Middlesex to declare three runs

Bob Gale attacks the Glamorgan bowling

ahead. Yorkshire collapsed in their second innings and Bennett (four for 29), Titmus (three for 39), Bedford (two for 48) and Gale (one wicket for no runs off four balls), bowled them out for 148, leaving Middlesex 146 in just over two and a half hours. Gale was caught by Illingworth off Platt without a run on the board, but Sid

> Alan Moss took only sixty-nine Championship wickets for Middlesex in 1962, compared with 112 the previous season to underline the strain imposed upon him through the lack of a really class opening partner.

Russell and Clarke put on 71 in fifty-five minutes and Middlesex won with about twenty minutes to spare.

The saddest moment of the year was in October when 'Patsy' Hendren died at the age of seventy-three. The brilliant batsman who was known for his Cockney wit and held in deep affection throughout the cricket world, was second only to Sir Jack Hobbs in the list of all-time century makers with 170 three-figure innings to his name, and third only to Hobbs and Frank Woolley with an aggregate of 57,610 first-class runs. From selling scorecards at Lord's, he continued his love of the game as a scorer. Lord's was his kingdom and he was its king.

FIRST CLASS RESULTS 1962
Championship Record

P	W	L	D	No Dcsn	Pos
28	6	8	13	1	13th

May
5-8   beat Somerset by ten wickets at Lord's
9-11   beat Cambridge University by 225 runs at Fenners
12-15   lost to Worcestershire by six wickets at Lord's
16-18   drew with Essex at Lord's
19-21   drew with Yorkshire at Middlesbrough
23-5   beat Oxford University by ten wickets at The Parks
26-8   lost to Gloucestershire by 45 runs at Stroud
May 30-1 **June** 1 lost to Hampshire by 62 runs at Lord's

June
2-5   beat Yorkshire by six wickets at Lord's
6-8   drew with Worcestershire at Worcester
9-12   lost to Sussex by six wickets at Lord's
13-15   beat Gloucestershire by 96 runs at Lord's
16-19   drew with Northamptonshire at Northampton
23-6   lost to Essex by ten wickets at Brentwood

June 30, **July** 2-3 drew with Glamorgan at Lord's
July
4-6   drew with Warwickshire at Nuneaton
11-13   lost to Kent by 84 runs at Dover
14-17   beat Leicestershire by 25 runs at Lord's
18-20   drew with Glamorgan at Newport
21-4   drew with the Pakistanis at Lord's
25-7   drew with Nottinghamshire at Lord's
28-31   lost to Surrey by 151 runs at The Oval
August
1-3   drew with Lancashire at Blackpool
4-7   drew with Sussex at Hove
8-10   beat Somerset by innings and 51 runs at Weston-super-Mare
11-14   drew with Surrey at Lord's
15-17   drew with Hampshire at Portsmouth
22-4   drew with Warwickshire at Lord's
25-8   lost to Derbyshire by eight wickets at Chesterfield
29-31   beat Lancashire by seven wickets at Lord's
September
1-4   no decision in match with Kent at Lord's

1963

Price of Success

Before the 1963 season began Middlesex cricket was saddened by the loss of another former player of epic stature, Sir Pelham Warner. He died on 30 January, aged eighty-nine, and with him went a great part of the county's past. In the same year, another great batsman died when Sir Jack Hobbs of Surrey passed away in December aged eighty-one. On the field Middlesex found themselves with a new captain when Ian Bedford retired and Colin Drybrough took over for 1963. Although the distinction between amateur and professional cricketers — and all its attendant class differences — was finally expunged in 1963, tradition died hard at Middlesex and they appointed Drybrough,

the Oxford Blue amateur, in a move which harked back to bygone days.

Drybrough's first season as Middlesex skipper saw the side rise from thirteenth position to sixth and they were one of three counties to beat champions Yorkshire. Bob Gale did not play regularly because of business committments and Middlesex struggled hard to find an opening partner for Eric Russell. The absence of the left-handed Gale was acutely felt. In 1962 he had scored well over 1,700 runs. He played only half the Championship games in 1963 and scored only 570 runs. Middlesex never managed to plug the gap left by the absence of Gale and although Parfitt, White, Eric Russell and Hooker all surpassed the 1,000-run mark — and Titmus might have also done, had he not missed nine games, mostly through Test calls — Middlesex had little of the batting stability of earlier years.

Bob White was perhaps the most improved player, scoring 700 more runs than in 1962 and being awarded his county cap in a season when he scored two centuries. White was tried as an opener but, good batsman though he was, he did not command the temperament and technique of a regular opener; Sid Russell was also tried but he, too, never gave Middlesex a sure sign that he was their answer. He averaged less than 20 runs in his seventeen innings.

Like most counties, Middlesex suffered from the weather in 1963. Three games were washed out before the first innings issue could be decided; and altogether, half of the Championship matches were undecided. The conditions favoured bowlers and it was a good time for a young paceman called John Price to burst upon the county scene. Price, born at Harrow, played a few games in 1961. Now he played in all the Championship matches and took eighty wickets at 22.21, a performance which earned him a place on the MCC tour to India that winter. Price was

Peter Parfitt is out for 22 in the first innings at The Oval

In the new Gillette Cup of 1963, Middlesex reached the second round with a 39-run win over Gloucestershire at Bristol. Middlesex were all out for 170 in 64.3 overs (the competition was of 65 overs per side) and then dismissed Gloucestershire for 131 in 51.5 overs. In the second round at Lord's, Middlesex were all out for 129 in 40.1 overs (Larter and Milburn taking four wickets each) and Northants knocked off the runs for the loss of four wickets in 39 overs. Colin Milburn scored 84 with one 6 and fifteen 4s.

the opening partner for whom Alan Moss had been searching since the retirement of John Warr. Sadly, this was to be Moss's last season. He took seventy-nine Championship wickets at 15.92, by far the best, discounting Peter Parfitt's seventeen victims for 13.47 each which put him technically on top of the bowling averages. Moss retired at the age of thirty-two, fourth in the English averages and able to go on for some time to come in the eyes of disappointed Middlesex members. Titmus

Bob White hits out at David Allen of Gloucestershire. The wicketkeeper is Barry Meyer, now a Test umpire

again did splendidly with seventy-two Championship wickets. Bennett, Hooker, Bick and Drybrough supported well and Ted Clark found himself catapulted up the averages on the strength of six wickets for 104 off 38 overs.

Middlesex were always around the middle of the table, although a dark period between 15 June and 19 July, when their only victory in nine games was the unexpected win over Yorkshire at Headingley, threatened to send them down to the basement of the Championship table. The game against Sussex at Lord's saw Middlesex lose by a single run in Fred Titmus's benefit match when Alan Oakman took the last three Middlesex second innings wickets, all leg-before, in the extra half-hour; Moss took eight wickets for 40 runs when Gloucestershire were skittled for 86 at Lord's; and the highlight of the match against the West Indians was an opening stand of 206 between McMorris (190 not out) and Hunte (103) as the tourists went on to win by nine wickets. McMorris's innings — he carried his bat through the West Indian's first innings — contained twenty-one 4s and lasted six hours and forty minutes.

But the most bizarre moment of the season came on the Monday morning of the match with Kent at Tunbridge Wells. On the Saturday, Kent were dismissed for 150 and at the close Middlesex had reached 121 for three. On the Monday, only the not-out batsman, Bob White, Sid Russell, who had already been dismissed, and twelfth man Ted Clark were at the ground when the game was due to start. The rest of the team had not arrived back from their weekend in London. Kent took the field but no batsmen appeared and eventually umpires 'Lofty' Herman and 'Dusty' Rhodes decreed that the Middlesex innings had been declared closed. Kent agreed to Clark keeping wicket while Sid Russell and Bob White opened the bowling, helped by eight Kent substitutes. By the start of the Kent innings, more players had arrived and Middlesex started with five substitutes. Ultimately rain curtailed the match.

FIRST CLASS RESULTS 1963
Championship Record

P	W	L	D	No Dcsn	Pos
28	9	5	11	3	6th

May

4-7   beat Nottinghamshire by 126 runs at Lord's

8-10   drew with Oxford University at The Parks

11-14   beat Cambridge University by eight wickets at Fenners

15-17   lost to Kent by 50 runs at Lord's

25-8   drew with Worcestershire at Lord's

29-31   beat Northants by ten wickets at Lord's

June

1-4   lost to Sussex by one run at Lord's

5-7   lost to Hampshire by 99 runs at Lord's

8-11   beat Essex by 158 runs at Lord's

15-18   drew with Kent at Tunbridge Wells

19-21   drew with Nottinghamshire at Worksop

22-5   drew with Northants at Peterborough

26-8   drew with Essex at Southend

June 29, **July** 1-2 drew with Warwickshire at Lord's

July

3-5   no decision in game with Derbyshire at Ilkeston

6-9   beat Yorkshire by six wickets at Headingley

13-16   drew with Gloucestershire at Gloucester

17-19   lost to Lancashire by six wickets at Southport

20-3   lost to West Indies by nine wickets at Lord's

27-9   beat Lancashire by 256 runs at Lord's

July 31,**August** 1 beat Hampshire by innings and 89 runs at Portsmouth

August

3-5   drew with Sussex at Hove

7-9   beat Somerset by one wicket at Weston-super-Mare

10-13   lost to Surrey by eight wickets at The Oval

14-16   no decision in match with Glamorgan at Lord's

17-20   drew with Yorkshire at Lord's

21-3   drew with Leicestershire at Leicester

24-7   beat Worcestershire by 61 runs at Worcester

28-30   beat Gloucestershire by six wickets at Lord's

August 31, **September** 2-3 drew with Surrey at Lord's

September

4-6   no decision in match with Derbyshire at Lord's

Gillette Cup

May

22   beat Gloucestershire by 39 runs in first round at Bristol

June

12   lost to Northants by six wickets in second round at Lord's

1964

No Centenary Celebrations

Middlesex again finished sixth in the Championship but their first win at Lord's did not come until Leicestershire were beaten there, halfway though July. It was Drybrough's last season as captain and he suffered from having a side that was weak in bowling. John Price topped the England Test averages in the winter tour of India, but in 1964 he did not maintain the promise he had shown in his first full season, claiming only sixty Championship wickets at 26.10. Price won a place in two Tests against the Australians in 1964 but his form for Middlesex was disappointing. Only Fred Titmus, who topped the county's Championship averages with 101 wickets at 16.06 each, looked in good fettle. Bennett, Hooker and Drybrough were the other main bowlers, but the attack was usually not in keeping with the Middlesex batting which excelled in 1964.

Eric Russell scored 2,050 in the Championship alone — the first time for some years that a Middlesex batsman had achieved that feat — and he scored five centuries and topped the averages with 43.61. In all games he scored 2,342 runs and finished eighth in the national averages. Russell had a magnificent season. His 193 at Bournemouth was the highest of his career and he showed himself to be a batsman of the highest class with his fluent run-getting. Peter Parfitt missed twelve games through injury and Test calls but he still reached 1,000 in the Championship, scored 200 not out at Trent Bridge, and made five centuries, one of them for Middlesex against the Australians.

Mike Brearley topped the Cambridge University averages with 1,313 runs, four centuries, and a top score of 169, all of which gave him an average of 57.08. When the Cambridge season was over he joined Middlesex and, with Russell, formed one of the best opening partnerships in England at that time. Brearley scored 677 runs in the Championship at an average of 32.33, topping 2,000 runs in all first-class games in 1964 and finishing the season

Mike Smith about to catch his Surrey namesake W. A. Smith at The Oval

Russell takes runs off the Notts bowling at Lord's

When Peter Parfitt scored 101 against Surrey at The Oval in August 1964, Surrey's young pace bowler Geoff Arnold, later to play for England, had trouble with his front foot and on four successive occasions he pulled up in his delivery.

---

tenth in the English averages. There was pleasing news of Mike Smith, too. Smith scored his maiden first-class century at Hove and made 743 runs in thirty Championship innings. Yet he was still unsure of his place and would have to wait a while longer for a regular spot. Brearley, a useful wicketkeeper on his day (although Murray's excellence made that skill superfluous at Middlesex) played himself into the winter tour of South Africa with MCC. Sadly it was a poor tour for the young batsman and there was no hint of triumphs yet to come at Test level.

Middlesex's fielding had been one respect of the county's game which had not endured the ups and downs of the batting and bowling over the seasons. Hooker, Smith, Parfitt and Drybrough were specialists in the close positions and Middlesex rarely, if ever, lost a match for the want of holding their catches. One-day cricket had yet to improve fielding throughout the counties, but in 1964 the Middlesex groundwork was well-known and admired. In the Gillette Cup, however, it failed to take the county past the third round.

Middlesex's centenary season was not remarkable and they never looked likely candidates for honours, although for a two-week period in July they did rise to fourth place. Even Lord's proved an unhappy hunting ground and until they won three successive matches there, late in the season, they never looked happy at home. It was late in the season before Fred Titmus really found his form. Then, in the month of August, he had figures of seven for 70 against Surrey, six for 42 against Worcestershire, nine for 57 against Lancashire, and seven for 73 against Derbyshire. In between Titmus's glorious spell, Colin Drybrough enjoyed his own moment of glory at Northampton when he took four wickets in five balls and finished with seven for 94, although he could not prevent Northants winning by ten wickets.

The game against the Australians at Lord's was highlighted by centuries from Parfitt (121) and Brearley (106 not out). Middlesex declared at 285 for seven and the tourists replied with 347 for eight declared, Booth striking an elegant 132, which included twenty-one 4s before he was caught on the boundary by Price off Parfitt. Peter Burge was four short of his century when he fell to the same bowler. Parfitt's first innings century, which came in just under five hours, was followed by Brearley's in three and three quarter hours. Drybrough declared at 240 for seven, setting the Australians 179 in ninety minutes. It was a target they, not unnaturally did not attempt and after losing two wickets for 22 runs, they batted out time.

FIRST CLASS RESULTS 1964
Championship Record

P	W	L	D	No Dcsn	Pos
28	9	6	12	1	6th

May
- 2-4   drew with Cambridge University at Fenners
- 6-8   beat Oxford University by ten wickets at The Parks
- 9-12   lost to Worcestershire by five wickets at Lord's
- 13-15   lost to Yorkshire by ten wickets at Headingley
- 16-19   drew with Sussex at Lord's
- 20-2   drew with Gloucestershire at Lord's
- 23-6   beat Nottinghamshire by ten wickets at Trent Bridge
- **May** 30, **June** 1-2 drew with Hampshire at Lord's

June
- 3-5   no decision in match with Somerset at Lord's
- 6-9   drew with Nottinghamshire at Lord's
- 10-12   drew with Yorkshire at Lord's
- 13-16   beat Derbyshire by 107 runs at Burton-upon-Trent
- 20-3   drew with Warwickshire at Edgbaston
- 27-30   lost to Essex by six wickets at Lord's

July
- 1-3   drew with Glamorgan at Cardiff
- 4-6   beat Essex by one wicket at Westcliff
- 8-10   beat Lancashire by 12 runs at Old Trafford
- 11-14   beat Leicestershire by 130 runs at Lord's
- 15-17   drew with Hampshire at Bournemouth
- 18-21   drew with the Australians at Lord's
- 22-4   beat Gloucestershire by ten wickets at Bristol
- 25-8   drew with Surrey at The Oval

August
- 1-4   drew with Sussex at Hove
- 5-7   drew with Kent at Canterbury
- 8-11   drew with Surrey at Lord's
- 12-14   lost to Northampton by ten wickets at Northampton
- 19-20   lost to Worcestershire by nine wickets at Kidderminster
- 22-5   lost to Kent by nine wickets at Lord's
- 26-7   beat Lancashire by innings and 6 runs at Lord's
- **August** 29-31, **September** 1 beat Northants by 145 runs at Lord's

September
- 2-4   beat Derbyshire by 86 runs at Lord's

Gillette Cup

May
- 27   beat Yorkshire by 61 runs in the second round at Lord's

June
- 24   lost to Surrey by 144 runs in the third round at The Oval

1965

One-Day Semi Finalists

With Colin Drybrough leaving Middlesex, Fred Titmus assumed the captaincy for 1965 and took the side to sixth place for the third consecutive season. Apart from a purple patch in the latter half of June and well into July, when they reached the top of the table for a spell, Middlesex were never likely candidates for the Championship and after a poor finish they were perhaps a shade fortunate to maintain their position of the previous two summers. Of their last seventeen matches, Middlesex won only two, also losing to the South Africans and being knocked out of the semi-final of the Gillette Cup by Surrey at The Oval. How different to that earlier spell when they beat the eventual champions, Worcestershire, sent Gillette Cup holders Sussex spinning out of the competition, and enjoyed successive victories against Gloucestershire and against Glamorgan who were to finish third that season.

Once again Middlesex's main problem was the lack of bowling penetration. John Price was dogged by injury and played in only twelve Championship games, taking just thirty-three wickets, and Bob Hooker became the county's leading Championship wicket-taker with eighty-six, although they cost him over 24 runs apiece. Don Bennett opened the bowling in some matches and took fifty-four wickets at exactly 24 runs each, and newcomer Bob Herman, son of the former Hampshire fast bowler 'Lofty' Herman, showed some promise in his first season, taking twenty-seven wickets at 35.18. Fred Titmus was again the mainstay with seventy-five Championship victims at 16.90 each, to top the table; Bick was used more often and his off-spinners earned him fifty-one wickets and his county cap after some years on the staff; and Harry Latchman, a leg-spinner from Jamaica, showed promise with seventeen wickets at 20 runs each.

Surrey skipper Mickey Stewart looks disgusted after being clean bowled by Titmus during the Gillette Cup semi-final at The Oval

Titmus and Parfitt both missed several games, being involved with the Tests against New Zealand and South Africa, although Parfitt still found time to score 1,242 runs, with three centuries, to average a handsome 47.76 in the Championship and head the county's averages. Eric Russell had a fine season and scored 1,724 Championship runs, and Ted Clark continued his improvement with 1,352. Bob Gale played in fourteen games and managed 680 runs, and new boy Clive Radley was the most successful of the younger generation of Middlesex batsmen with an

who made an unbeaten 34, and Bob White (36 not out), paved the way to a second declaration at 174 for six, setting Nottinghamshire 299 in four hours and forty minutes. Nottinghamshire started with a stand of 119 in two and a quarter hours but then wickets fell rapidly and after Titmus broke through with four victims, Bennett mopped up the tail.

In the Gillette Cup Middlesex went into to the semi-finals for the first time. In the first round they met a Minor County side for the first time in competitive cricket when Buckinghamshire came to Lord's

Poor Stewart! At Lord's he drops Bick off Geoff Arnold's bowling

average of 29.37 from 470 runs. Mike Harris, a Cornishman who was inevitably nicknamed 'Pasty', played in five games but achieved nothing of note.

Titmus skippered the side confidently and in this first season he always seemed prepared to play positive cricket. No where was this more obvious than in the second Championship match of the season when Middlesex beat Nottinghamshire at Lord's by five runs with just four minutes to spare. Ted Clark paved the way for a declaration in the first innings with a career-best 122. Brearley, who was to have a fairly lean 1965 following the disappointments of a South African tour, made 44 and Middlesex closed at 312 for six. Don Bennett struck with six wickets as Nottinghamshire folded to 188 all out, and then brisk batting by Titmus,

and were soundly beaten by 158 runs. Bob Gale included two 6s and thirteen 4s in his 86 as Middlesex powered to 269; then Price and Hooker each took three wickets as Buckinghamshire were dismissed for 111 in just 38.1 overs. In the second round against Derbyshire, also at Lord's, the

During the match with Glamorgan at Lord's on 20 August 1965, the Glamorgan batsman A. Rees was given out 'handled the ball' in the Welshmen's second innings. It was the first time that this decision had been given in English first-class cricket since A. D. Nourse (senior) suffered a similar fate when batting for the South Africans against Sussex at Hove in July 1907.

margin was much narrower and Middlesex won a tense match by 10 runs. Don Bennett took four wickets as Derbyshire ran out of overs at 151 for eight with Bob Taylor taking the Man of the Match award with three catches and an unbeaten 53. Taylor and Harold Rhodes had put on the highest stand of the game — 74 — when the 60 overs were up.

Middlesex's finest win came on 23 June when they beat holders Sussex by 90 runs. John Murray hit one 6 and five 4s in his 49; Bob Gale scored a brilliant 74 and Peter Parfitt made 66 as Middlesex stormed to 280 for eight. Sussex needed well over four an over, but after some early scares when Ken Suttle and Ted Dexter broke loose, Titmus put the brake on Sussex while Bennett broke through with four wickets to give Middlesex a place in the last four. Sadly, Middlesex went no further and Surrey beat them by five wickets at The Oval. The game was, however, a victory for cricket. Over 500 runs were scored in the day and Middlesex's total of 250 was due to some frantic batting late in their innings after only 77 runs had come off the first 32 overs. Eric Russell (70) and Brearley (60) were Middlesex's highest scorers. Surrey made the runs they needed for victory off 56.2 overs, thanks to John Edrich (71), Ken Barrington (68 not out) and M. J. Edwards (53 not out) who took the Man of the Match award for his part in a 92-run stand with Barrington in just ten overs.

FIRST CLASS RESULTS 1965
Championship Record

P	W	L	D	No Dcsn	Pos
28	8	7	12	1	6th

May

1-4 drew with Oxford University at The Parks

5-7 drew with Kent at Lord's

8-11 beat Cambridge University by ten wickets at Fenners

12-14 beat Nottinghamshire by 5 runs at Lord's

15-18 lost to Somerset by nine wickets at Bristol

19-21 drew with Northants at Lord's

May 29-31, **June** 1 drew with Somerset at Lord's

June

2-4 beat Lancashire by seven wickets at Lord's

5-8 drew with Sussex at Lord's

9-11 lost to Derbyshire by five wickets at Chesterfield

12-15 beat Lancashire by nine wickets at Old Trafford

16-18 beat Worcestershire by five wickets at Worcester

19-21 lost to Leicestershire by ten wickets at Loughborough

26-9 beat Gloucestershire by nine wickets at Lord's

June 30, **July** 1 beat Glamorgan by ten wickets at Swansea

July

3-6 drew with Hampshire at Lord's

7-9 drew with Hampshire at Southampton

10-13 drew with Worcestershire at Lord's

17-20 drew with Surrey at The Oval

21-3 drew with Yorkshire at Scarborough

28-30 drew with Northants at Northampton

July 31, **August** 2-3 beat Sussex by nine wickets at Hove

August

4-6 lost to Kent by 76 runs at Canterbury

7-10 lost to Surrey by 34 runs at Lord's

11-13 lost to the South Africans by five wickets at Lord's

14-17 beat Leicestershire by seven wickets at Lord's

18-20 drew with Glamorgan at Lord's

21-4 no decision in the game with Yorkshire at Lord's

25-7 lost to Warwickshire by innings and 38 runs at Edgbaston

28-31 lost to Essex by nine wickets at Leyton

September

1-3 drew with Warwickshire at Lord's

Gillette Cup

April

23 beat Buckinghamshire by 158 runs in the first round at Lord's

May

22 beat Derbyshire by 10 runs in the second round at Lord's

June

23 beat Sussex by 90 runs in the third round at Lord's

July

14 lost to Surrey by five wickets in the semi-final at The Oval

1966

Middlesex Without Teeth

Despite losing only five matches — the same number as champions Yorkshire — Middlesex tumbled down the table to finish equal twelfth in 1966. The reason was that they simply could not bowl out their opponents and even though John Price returned to something like his old form with ninety Championship victims at 18.65 runs each, the bowling still gave cause for concern. Bob Herman's action showed a much lower arm after he had been coached into abandoning his classic high action because he could not get the ball to move through the air, and his effectiveness was greatly diminished because of this. Hooker took only fifty-five wickets in the Championship, thirty-one fewer than in 1965, although he missed seven games through the back injury which eventually forced him to retire, and Titmus was also less effective. The captain lost his Test place during the season and failed to take 100 wickets for the first time since 1960. A brighter spot was the form of West Indian fast-medium bowler, Wes Stewart, signed from Gloucester-

> In 1966 the first innings of 102 County Championship matches were restricted to 65 overs. They were the first twelve games played by each side on a home and away basis. Where counties met only once in the season normal conditions applied. The experiment was not a success.

shire early in the season, who gave Price admirable support with sixty-four wickets at 22.42 each.

In the batting Parfitt was head and shoulders above the rest of his colleagues with 1,860 championship runs, two centuries, and an average of 44.28. Only Ted Clark and Eric Russell joined Parfitt on the four-figure mark and Titmus, as well as having an indifferent season with the ball, also failed with the bat and scored only 530 runs at 19.62. Russell's form suffered after two indifferent Tests against West Indies (scores of 26, 20, 4, 11) and he was not helped by a succession of opening partners. Only Mike Harris showed real promise with 767 runs in his fifteen games. John Murray, out for a month with a foot injury, never reproduced the batting form which gave him two centuries against West Indies for Egland and MCC.

One of the most thrilling and entertaining matches of the whole Middlesex season came at Weston-super-Mare at the end of July when Fred Titmus took his first-ever hat-trick and Ron Hooker scored a brilliant century on a quite awful pitch. Hooker's amazing century came in a match that was otherwise dominated by bowlers on the dry and badly-worn pitch. Hooker reached his century in eighty-nine minutes and was finally out for 102 (one 6 and thirteen 4s). The rest of the batting collapsed and it was only due to Hooker, who went in at 110 for five, that Middlesex reached 239 all out.

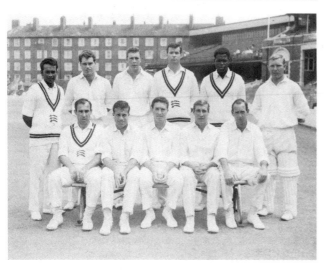

Middlesex 1966: Back row left to right: Latchman, Clark, Harris, Price, Stewart, Clifton. Front row: Hooker, Bennett, Titmus, Parfitt, Russell

Bick is bowled out by Ken Higgs (Lancashire) for a single while his stump flies past the close fielder

Somerset replied with 158, thanks mainly to Langford's lusty 55 in eighty-two minutes after the home side slid to 80 for eight. When Middlesex batted again only Ted Clark came to terms with the now desperately difficult conditions and he scored 35 before being caught by Palmer off Langford, after a particularly severe attack on Rumsey. Brian Langford mopped up Middlesex with six for 60 and they were all out for 126, leaving Somerset to score 208 for victory. Inside one hour the entire Somerset side were back in the dressing room after being bowled out for 43. John Price took six for 12 and Titmus took the first hat-trick of his career, which began, ironically, against Somerset at Bath in 1949.

The Somerset victory was one of only six matches won in the Championship. The Middlesex record at Lord's was uncharacteristically indifferent. They did not win their first match there until Sussex were soundly beaten at Whitsun in John Murray's benefit match. And Middlesex failed to win at home again after the end of June. Even the usually superb Middlesex fielding was not up to its usual high standard, although Parfitt did top the national catching list with forty-eight chances accepted altogether

The game against the West Indians was drawn, although on the last day Middlesex were near to beating a touring side for the first time in thirty years. West Indians gave an excruciating display of batting on the first day, scoring only 187 off 95.2 overs. They declared overnight and Charlie Griffiths grabbed four quick wickets as Middlesex tumbled to 42 for five before Clark and Hooker came to the rescue with a stand of 131 before Clark, looking for the single that would give him his century, was stumped by Allan off Carew. Hooker continued to 81 before he was out and Titmus declared soon after at 243 for eight. Middlesex captured three wickets before close of play, another in the early stages of the following day, and just after lunch the tourists were 110 ahead. Butcher and Brancker added 72 in less than an hour and when the West Indians were all out for 242, Middlesex needed 187 in two hours and twenty minutes. After West Indies took over a quarter of an hour to bowl their first three overs, the task looked even more difficult; when bad light held up play for ten minutes just before tea, it proved impossible.

FIRST CLASS RESULTS 1966
Championship Record

P	W	L	D	No Dcsn	Pos
28	6	5	14	3	12th=

April 30, **May** 2-3 beat Cambridge University by 232 runs at Fenners

May

4-6 no decision in the match with Warwickshire at Edgbaston

7-10 lost to Kent by 117 runs at Lord's

11-13 drew with Glamorgan at Lord's

14-17 drew with Kent at Gravesend

18-20 drew with Warwickshire at Lord's

25-7 drew with Leicester at Lord's

28-31 beat Sussex by seven wickets at Lord's

June

1-2 beat Oxford University by innings and 11 runs at The Parks

4-7 drew with Yorkshire at Lord's

8-10 beat Somerset by six wickets at Lord's

11-14 drew with Worcestershire at Worcester

15-17 drew with Leicestershire at Leicester

18-21 drew with Nottinghamshire at Trent Bridge

25-8 beat Northants by nine wickets at Lord's

July

2-5 drew with Glamorgan at Cardiff

6-8 drew with the West Indians at Lord's

9-12 lost to Surrey by 105 runs at The Oval

13-15 drew with Derbyshire at Lord's

16-19 drew with Essex at Lord's

23-6 lost to Yorkshire by 120 runs at Sheffield

27-8 beat Somerset by 164 runs at Weston-super-Mare

July 30, **August** 1-2 beat Northants by six wickets at Northampton

August

3-5 no decision in the match with Lancashire at Old Trafford

6-9 drew with Surrey at Lord's

13-16 drew with Lancashire at Lord's

17-19 lost to Hampshire by 80 runs at Bournemouth

20-3 beat Gloucestershire by nine wickets at Cheltenham

24-5 lost to Worcestershire by innings and 41 runs at Lord's

27-30 drew with Sussex at Hove

August 31, **September** 1-2 no decision in the match with Hampshire at Lord's

Gillette Cup

May

21 lost to Lancashire by 63 runs in the second round at Lord's

1967

The Big Yawn

Middlesex won no friends in 1967. Their singularly unattractive brand of cricket, particularly at Lord's, was quite out of keeping with the traditions of the club. Four games were doomed to no decision — one of them the match against Gloucestershire at Lord's in late May when not a ball could be bowled due to rain — but the weather was not to blame for every stalemate. Against Hampshire at Lord's in early July there was again no decision — yet only a few minutes play had been lost in the entire three days. There was no hint of the drudgery to come when Roy Marshall scored a brilliant century for Hampshire. His 153 included one 6 and eighteen 4s and was scored out of a Hampshire total of 210 in only three hours and twenty-three minutes.

But after that exciting start, the Hampshire innings was becalmed. Livingstone made an unbeaten 120 in four hours and ten minutes and Hampshire ground on into the second day before declaring at 421 for seven. It was the first-ever Sunday of county cricket at Lord's but after Middlesex lost Eric Russell and Mike Harris with only 29 on the board, they too became entrenched. They had, of course, no chance of winning the match after Hampshire's long innings, but they never gave the crowd value for money. At the start of the last day Middlesex still needed 148 to avoid following-on and Radley and Hooker saw them beyond that point. But when Hooker was stumped for 66, Titmus ordered that Hampshire should be denied first innings points. Radley made 100 not out in Middlesex's 371 for seven at the close.

It was ironic that towards the end of the season the same two sides should set up an exciting match at Portsmouth which resulted in the first tie in the Champion-

Middlesex skipper Fred Titmus makes a great catch to dismiss his Surrey counterpart Mickey Stewart at The Oval

ship for eight years. Mike Smith's 135 not out set Middlesex up for a declaration at 327 for five. Hampshire lost Reed with five runs on the board and although Gilliatt and Marshall shared a brisk stand, the home team were deep in trouble until eighteen-year-old D. R. Turner came to their rescue with 87 in 165 minutes to take his side to exactly 50 behind on first innings. Middlesex second innings' wickets fell cheaply, despite Radley (46 not out), Russell (30) and Smith (23), and acting skipper Murray declared at 123 for seven, setting Hampshire 174 in two hours.

At 100 for three Hampshire were on course for victory but when Middlesex captured three wickets with the score unchanged at 154, the match was finely balanced. Wheatley scored a valuable 28 before being run out and with the last over to play, Sainsbury was still there with Cottam. Three runs were still needed for Hampshire to win when Herman started that final over. Middlesex needed just one wicket to make certain of victory. Two runs came off Herman's first five balls and as he ran in to deliver the last ball of a tense match, Hampshire needed just a single. Sainsbury, who had 11 runs to his

name, was stranded at the far end and he could only watch as Herman uprooted Cottam's wicket to make the result exactly equal.

Middlesex finished seventh in the table, an improvement of several places on 1966, but still a long way short of the kind of success which supporters wanted from their distinguished club. Even two victor-

> In a three-week spell during June 1967, Mike Harris amassed 692 runs in nine innings. Clive Radley was two runs short of 1,000 in Championship games, although he scored 1,057 in all matches. Mike Smith notched 894 in the Championship and 1,065 in all games.

ies in the first two games, and an early innings defeat of Yorkshire when Parfitt scored 134 and Titmus took seven wickets in the Yorkshiremen's first innings, did not help them. After losing at Blackheath in June Middlesex won only two more Championship matches, thanks partly to their caution. In fairness, it has to be pointed out that once again Titmus had problems with the side's bowling. Price and Hooker again missed games through injury and Price played in only one match during a two-month spell in mid-season. Titmus regained some of his cutting skills, as did Herman, and the Middlesex skipper did the double for the first time since 1962. His Championship haul of ninety wickets put him on top of the Middlesex averages at a cost of 19.76 each. Herman was the next-highest wicket taker (sixty-eight), followed by Harry Latchman (who played in every game and took forty-seven wickets with his leg spinners), Wes Stewart (forty-five), Price (forty-three), Parfitt (used as a second off-spinner and capturing thirty-seven wickets), and Hooker (thirty-two).

Mike Harris joined Eric Russell in one of the best opening partnerships in the county. The Cornishman scored 1,463 runs and was third in the averages behind Parfitt (1,520) and Russell (1,498). Ted Clark's premature retirement caused a problem and Murray's elevation in the order did nothing to solve it. In the match against the Pakistanis, Russell (167) and

Mike Willett is caught Murray bowled Latchman for 9 runs at The Oval

Harris (160) set a Middlesex record for the first wicket with a stand of 312; Russell was the first man in the country to 1,000 runs and Harris joined him during that innings against the tourists, winning his county cap into the bargain. In the same match Harry Latchman had career-best figures of seven for 91.

FIRST CLASS RESULTS 1967
Championship Record

P	W	L	D	Tie	No Dcsn	Pos
28	5	4	14	1	4	7th

May

6-9   beat Derbyshire by nine wickets at Lord's

10-12   beat Lancashire by 176 runs at Lord's

17-19   drew with Cambridge University at Fenners

20-3   **beat Oxford University by 269 runs at The Parks**

24-6   no decision in match with Gloucestershire at Lord's

27-30   no decision in match with Sussex at Lord's

June

3-6   beat Yorkshire by innings and 58 runs at Lord's

7-9   drew with Kent at Lord's

10-13   lost to Kent by six wickets at Blackheath

14-16   drew with Worcestershire at Lord's

17-19   drew with Nottinghamshire at Trent Bridge

21-3   drew with Warwickshire at Edgbaston

24-6   drew with Essex at Colchester

28-30   beat Worcestershire by four wickets at Worcester

July

1-3   no decision in game with Hampshire at Lord's

5-7   drew with the Pakistanis at Lord's

8-10   drew with Surrey at The Oval

12-14   drew with Yorkshire at Sheffield

15-17   beat Northants by eight wickets at Lord's

22-5   drew with Glamorgan at Swansea

26-8   drew with Lancashire at Old Trafford

29-31   lost to Northants by 79 runs at Northampton

August

2-4   lost to Gloucestershire by three wickets at Bristol

5-8   drew with Derbyshire at Derby

9-11   drew with Leicestershire at Lord's

12-25   **no decision in the match with Nottinghamshire at Lord's**

16-18   drew with Essex at Lord's

19-21   drew with Surrey at Lord's

23-5   tied with Hampshire at Portsmouth

26-9   drew with Sussex at Hove

August 30-1, **September** 1 lost to Somerset by ten wickets at Lord's

Gillette Cup

May

13   lost to Sussex by 31 runs in second round at Hove

1968

Parfitt's Bonus

Four Championship victories in the last four matches saw Middlesex rise from the depths of the table to tenth position. The late change coincided with the appointment of Peter Parfitt as skipper in place of Freddie Titmus who resigned the position having accepted that under his leadership Middlesex had become a boring side. Ironically, Titmus had a good season as a player in 1968, taking 100 wickets in the Championship, and heading the batting averages, although Middlesex's batting was so poor this season that to head the list was not so great an achievement as it would first appear. Indeed, Titmus's average was only 25.63 and the fact that this could not be bettered in Championship games spoke volumes for the indifferent form suffered by the other main batsmen. Only Russell and Parfitt edged past the 1,000-run mark, and only three Championship centuries were scored — by Murray, Parfitt and Harris.

This was the first season in which bonus points for batting and bowling were introduced (a bonus for runs over 150) and for wickets taken in the first 85 overs of each side's first innings). Middlesex claimed only twenty-one batting points, the lowest tally of any team in the Championship. The standard of the Lord's pitches had fallen sharply and one man who suffered greatly was Harris who, despite his century, struggled for most of the season, particularly when on the back foot, and was eventually dropped to make way for Mike Smith as Russell's opening partner, although Smith, too, did little of note. It was Harris's last season at Lord's. He went to Nottinghamshire on special registration and found a new career at Trent Bridge as a prolific scorer.

If the Middlesex batting was frail in 1968, there was little wrong with the side's bowling. John Price had a fine season and topped the averages with eighty-eight

T. M. Cordaroy played only three innings for Middlesex and in this one he makes the Surrey close fielders take evasive action as he attempts to sweep Pat Pocock at The Oval

A youthful Mike Brearley turns a ball from Northants' Scott and is well caught by an equally young-looking David Steele

Championship wickets at 16.45 each, and we have already seen that Titmus was back to top form, recovering well from a boating accident in Barbados in February when he lost four toes during the MCC tour to the West Indies. Parfitt, Herman and Hooker all took useful wickets while Wes Stewart slipped quietly from the Middlesex scene with just twelve victims at 32.66 each. But the bowling revelation of 1968, so far as Middlesex were concerned, was little Harry Latchman. The sight of the cheery fellow from Kingston tossing up his leg-breaks — and claiming eighty-one Championship wickets — was one of the more pleasant aspects of the season. In an age when the leg-spinner was becoming an endangered species, Latchman went a long way to becoming the best of those left.

Middlesex's early games were disasterous. Five times they failed to win games when they were batting against the clock. And away from Lord's they suffered three defeats in June, including two games — against Yorkshire and Essex — lost inside two days. The first win did not come until Sussex were beaten at Lord's on 4 June and until Parfitt took over the reins, the fortunes of Middlesex looked like finishing at their lowest point for many years. Only in the Gillette Cup was there some relief when Middlesex went to the semi-finals before losing to the eventual winners, Warwickshire, in a game held over from the originally allotted three days due to rain.

Middlesex's poor batting in 1968 is graphically illustrated by the top of the Championship averages.					
	Inn	No	Runs	HS	Ave
Titmus	37	4	846	75	25.63
Murray	37	4	831	104*	25.18
Russell	47	1	1150	91	25.00
Parfitt	48	6	1050	131*	25.00
Radley	45	8	904	99	24.43
Brearley	21	3	437	82*	24.27
Smith	44	6	864	84	22.73
Harris	26	3	516	109	22.43
*denotes not out innings.					

The second game of Middlesex's four-match run-in at the end of the season proved to be remarkable. On the first two days of the match with Kent — played on a lively Lord's 'greentop' which reminded older supporters and players of the sort of wickets prepared at HQ a decade or more before — 251 runs were scored while twenty-four wickets fell. On the last day there was a complete transformation and 452 runs were scored for the loss of only eight wickets. Middlesex were set 235 in three hours. At 120 for six — and with just over an hour to play — Middlesex looked on the ropes. Then Colin Cowdrey was hit for 24 runs in three overs and Middlesex got home one minute from the close. Hooker (73 not out) and Titmus (38 not out) added 115 in that last hour.

The Australian match could have been a real thriller, but for the rain. Peter

Parfitt scored a fine undefeated 110 in Middlesex's first innings to follow up the century he made for the county against the 1964 Australians. Parfitt and Radley (70 not out) enjoyed an unbroken stand of 165 in three hours and fifteen minutes before Titmus declared at 277 for four. The Australians were never happy against the off-spin of Titmus and Parfitt and managed only 227. Middlesex could not press home their advantage. Eight wickets fell for 108 — six of them to Renneberg — when rain halted play with the county 158 ahead. There were a number of possible outcomes. In the end, the weather won yet again.

FIRST CLASS RESULTS 1968
Championship Record

P	W	L	D	Pos
28	8	6	14	10th

May
1-3 drew with Derbyshire at Derby
8-11 drew with Nottinghamshire at Trent Bridge
11-14 drew with Gloucestershire at Lord's
15-16 beat Oxford University by innings and 213 runs at The Parks
18-20 drew with Hampshire at Bournemouth
22-4 drew with Lancashire at Lord's
20-31 drew with Glamorgan at Lord's
June
1-4 beat Sussex by three wickets at Lord's
8-11 drew with Essex at Lord's
12-14 beat Nottinghamshire by ten wickets at Lord's
15-17 lost to Lancashire by four wickets at Old Trafford
19-20 lost to Yorkshire by innings and 156 runs at Headingley
22-4 lost to Essex by 88 runs at Southend
26-8 drew with Kent at Tunbridge Wells
June 29-30, **July** 1 beat Surrey by seven wickets at Lord's
July
6-9 drew with Leicestershire at Leicester
13-15 drew with Surrey at The Oval
17-19 lost to Warwickshire by innings and two runs at Lord's
20-3 drew with the Australians at Lord's
24-6 lost to Northants by 27 runs at Lord's
27-9 beat Somerset by 29 runs at Weston-super-Mare
July 31, **August** 1-2 drew with Gloucestershire at Bristol
August
3-6 drew with Hampshire at Lords
10-12 lost to Yorkshire by 117 runs at Lord's
14-16 drew with Northants at Northampton
17-19 drew with Worcestershire at Worcester
21-3 beat Derbyshire by six wickets at Lord's
28-30 beat Kent by four wickets at Lord's
August 31, **September** 2-3 beat Sussex by 161 runs at Hove
September
4-6 beat Worcestershire by nine wickets at Lord's

Gillette Cup
May
4-6 beat Essex by 6 runs in first round at Lord's
25-7 beat Surrey by 103 runs in second round at Lord's
July
3 beat Leicestershire by 18 runs in third round at Lord's
August
13 lost to Warwickshire by three wickets in semi-final at Lord's

1969

...And Parfitt's Burden

The burden which Peter Parfitt had to bear during his first full season as captain of Middlesex was a full one. It was a burden which was not eased by the fact that Parfitt's captaincy was not confirmed for some time, a situation which must have added to the strain he picked up after taking over from Titmus in midstream the previous season. In addition to the insecurity of his position, Parfitt also had to contend with leading a side frail in batting and lacking in penetrative bowling. Only three games were won in the Championship, and two of those were against Northants and Somerset, neither side being noted for its ability to bowl out the opposition. Indeed, Middlesex's first success did not come until the second week in July when they defeated Northants by one wicket at Lord's. Apart from the six-wicket win over Somerset — who were to finish bottom of the Championship in 1969 — the only other success was a 34-run win over Gloucestershire.

The defeat was a crushing blow to Gloucestershire's hopes of the Championship and was part of a Middlesex hat-trick of upsets against title contenders. They drew twice with Hampshire and once with Surrey to thwart their chances and open up the way for Glamorgan to take their first county Championship since their only other success in 1948. In a low-scoring match Gloucestershire needed 259 in five hours for a crucial victory. Gloucestershire started badly, losing three wickets for 24 runs, picked up when Nicholls and Bissex, and then Nicholls and Brown, came together. But when Price got rid of Nicholls with the second new ball, Connolly mopped up the last three batsmen to finish with four for 31.

Alan Connolly, the Australian pace bowler who had done so well on the 1968 tour, taking twenty-three Test wickets at 21.34, was leading wicket-taker in Middlesex's Championship side with seventy-four at 22.68. But he failed to reproduce

Australia's Alan Connelly in action for Middlesex

the form which had worried England's Test batsmen the previous summer. That he ended the Gloucestershire innings with the second new ball was typical of him in 1969 and he often looked more dangerous the second time around. Poor John Price had a worrying season. He took only half the number of wickets he claimed in 1968 and on only one occasion did he manage five wickets in an innings. Even Fred Titmus did not manage three wickets in an innings until July, though he picked up to finish with fifty-nine Championship scalps, and Ron Hooker struggled to average slightly over one wicket per match in his fifteen games. Keith Jones, born at Park Royal, showed some pot-

Norman Featherstone, a young Rhodesian who some purists thought too impetuous for regular county cricket. He answered them by scoring nearly 9,000 runs for Middlesex

Norman Featherstone's first Championship match saw him score 30 and 51. But he was still on the losing side as Middlesex went down by an innings against Nottinghamshire at Lord's in June 1969.

ential with twenty-two wickets from 170 overs of medium-pace inswingers, but Harry Latchman struggled and was finally left out of the side.

Only Clive Radley exceeded 1,000 runs and his cover driving was a treat to behold. Another youngster, Rhodesian Norman Featherstone, came into the side in June and impressed, though some purists thought his style a shade too impetuous, and Mike Smith and Parfitt did adequately without ever covering themselves in sustained glory. Sadly, Eric Russell, in his benefit year, had a topsy-turvey season. He top-scored with 170 against Northants at Lord's, but endured a nightmarish month with six ducks in thirteen innings and went to pieces. Murray made 728 Championship runs without ever promising more; and Titmus could score only 384 — his lowest since 1950.

Middlesex drew their first three Championship games and their first definite results were both innings defeats at Lord's Kent dismissed them for 50 in the first innings of the match there in mid-May. Not one Middlesex player scraped into double figures as Derek Underwood (six for 22) and Bob Woolmer (four for 12) rattled them out. It was a feeble Middlesex performance, for there was little help for the Kent pair in the Lord's pitch. Luckhurst's century had taken Kent to 295 for seven declared and, following-on, Middlesex made a slightly better fight of it in their second innings, with the hard-hitting Jones making 48, but this time they had little answer to John Dye and were all out for 179. In the second such defeat, Nottinghamshire made 362 for eight declared (D. L. Murray 101) and then bowled out Middlesex for 101 and 194, Stead and Halfyard doing most of the damage.

The 1969 season saw the start of the 40-overs-a-side John Player League, abhorred by the purists but which proved to be one of cricket's life-savers over the ensuing years. Middlesex finished seventh in this new-style cricket and shared three records, two of them painful. They were dismissed for the lowest total — 50 by Worcestershire at Kidderminster — and were on the receiving end of the highest total — 288 for six by Sussex at Hove. The good news was Radley's 133 not out against Glamorgan, then the highest score in the John Player League. In the other one-day competition, the Gillette Cup, Middlesex got no further than the second round at Trent Bridge.

Championship Record

P	W	L	D	Pos
24	3	7	14	11th

May
- 3-6 drew with Essex at Lord's
- 7-9 drew with Warwickshire at Edgbaston
- 14-16 drew with Leicestershire at Lord's
- 17-20 lost to Kent by innings and 66 runs at Lord's
- 21-2 beat Oxford University by nine wickets at The Parks
- 24-7 drew with Sussex at Lord's

May 31, **June** 2-3 drew with Worcestershire at Dudley

June
- 4-6 lost to Nottinghamshire by innings and 67 runs at Lord's
- 11-13 beat Cambridge University by eight wickets at Fenners
- 14-17 drew with Yorkshire at Lord's
- 18-20 lost to Lancashire by 14 runs at Lord's
- 21-4 drew with Derbyshire at Burton-upon-Trent

July
- 5-8 beat Northants by one wicket at Lord's
- 9-11 drew with Essex at Westcliff
- 12-15 lost to Kent by five wickets at Canterbury
- 16-18 **drew with the New Zealanders at Lord's**
- 19-22 lost to Surrey by 183 runs at The Oval
- 23-4 lost to Northants by nine wickets at Kettering
- 26-9 drew with Lancashire at Old Trafford

August
- 2-5 beat Somerset by six wickets at Lord's
- 9-12 drew with Hampshire at Lord's
- 16-19 drew with Surrey at Lord's
- 20-2 lost to Glamorgan by three wickets at Swansea
- 23-6 drew with Hampshire at Bournemouth
- 27-9 beat Gloucestershire by 34 runs at Lord's

August 30, **September** 1-2, drew with Sussex at Hove

September
- 13-16 drew with Yorkshire at Harrogate

Gillette Cup

May
- 12 beat Buckinghamshire by 128 runs in the first round at Lord's

June
- 7 lost to Nottinghamshire by seven wickets in the second round at Trent Bridge

John Player League

April
- 27 beat Yorkshire by 27 runs at Lord's

May
- 4 beat Gloucestershire by 20 runs at Bristol
- 18 match with Nottinghamshire at Trent Bridge abandoned
- 25 beat Northants by 35 runs at Lord's

June
- 1 lost to Worcestershire by 60 runs at Kidderminster
- 15 lost to Essex by 21 runs at Ilford
- 22 lost to Derbyshire by six wickets at Derby

July
- 6 match with Leicestershire at Lord's abandoned
- 13 lost to Kent by seven wickets at Canterbury
- 20 beat Warwickshire by 9 runs at Lord's
- 27 lost to Lancashire by six wickets at Old Trafford

August
- 3 beat Somerset by 51 runs at Lord's
- 10 lost to Hampshire by seven wickets at Lord's
- 17 beat Surrey by 129 runs at Lord's
- 24 beat Glamorgan by 72 runs at Lord's
- 31 lost to Sussex by 57 runs at Hove

John Player League Record

P	W	L	T	NR	Pts	Pos
16	7	7	0	2	30	7th

1970

Darkest Days

Middlesex finished next to the bottom — their worst season since 1930. Indeed, only one point separated them from the bottom club, Gloucestershire, who went into their last match of the season needing only four points to avoid the wooden spoon but won only three. It was a tight thing but Middlesex's overall record was perhaps not that bad. Their five victories was a higher number than that achieved by five other counties in the Championship; and they lost only five. Where Middlesex foundered in 1970 was in the collection of bonus points. *Wisden* commented: 'Too often Middlesex gave the impression of waiting for a win to turn up without seeming to appreciate that ten or more points can be gathered by enterprising cricket in the first innings with the prospect then of ten more points for a win.'

When one considers that champions, Kent, had the same number of defeats as Middlesex, then that assessment rings very true. After the indifferent times of the previous few summers, 1970 can go down in the nadir of modern Middlesex cricket. Again the bowlers were largely to blame. John Price took seventy-seven Championship wickets at 23.50 to finish

top of the averages, but Alan Connolly missed a month of the season through injury — a back and a hamstring — and he took just forty-two wickets at 35.95 in his eighteen matches. Connolly maintained his place only because Bob Herman's progress was retarded. The Hampshire-born seamer played in only eight games and his 13 wickets were at a costly 40 runs apiece.

Connolly's contract was terminated by mutual consent after the 1970 season and another bowler who felt the cold wind of ill fortune was Harry Latchman who received a savage mauling from Hampshire's Roy Marshall in the opening match of the season at Lord's (where brilliant Marshall struck 189 — two 6s and twenty-three 4s — and shared in a new Hampshire fourth-wicket stand of 263). Harry Latchman then split a hand at Bristol in late June and did not play again that season. Peter Parfitt bowled himself more and took twenty-five wickets, while Fred Titmus took eighty-nine — more than any other player — and finished second in the averages to Price, the next-highest wicket-taker.

The Middlesex batting was in much better fettle and six players — Parfitt, Russell, Radley, Smith, Murray and Featherstone — all scored over 1,000 runs. The opening partnership of Mike Smith and Eric Russell was now slipping nicely into full gear and against Oxford University — albeit in a fairly meaningless match — they enjoyed opening stands of 131 and 140, the latter being unbroken as they set up Middlesex for a 130-runs win. Mike Brearley played in ten matches and averaged nearly 30 runs per innings. Mike Smith should have been the first batsman to 1,000 runs, but he suffered a 'pair' when he was just five runs short of the magic figure.

Although the bowling won few honours in 1970, there was one splendid performance against Kent at Lord's when John

Peter Parfitt is bowled by Pocock after he had scored 133 in the Middlesex second innings at The Oval

Owzat! Kent batsman Stuart Leary is left in no doubt that John Murray has caught him off the bowling of John Price at Lord's

Price took eight wickets in the first innings as Kent were rattled out for 110, and then followed up with six in the second to give himself match figures of fourteen wickets for 89. Kent were beaten comfortably and Middlesex — and Price — enjoyed a rare moment of glory in 1970. One other came when Yorkshire's Brian Close made a generous declaration at Lord's to leave Middlesex to score 247 in three hours and thirty-five minutes. Mike Smith saw Middlesex through to 195 for six, having batted brilliantly for his 118 which included one 6 and twelve 4s. Murray and Jones kept the runs up with the clock and when Murray was bowled out by Richard Hutton for 39, Middlesex were almost home. Still the runs came and Jones clubbed the penultimate ball of the match back past Tony Nicholson for a boundary and Middlesex won by three wickets.

The Gillette Cup first round brought Bill Edrich back to Lord's. At the age of fifty-four, Edrich returned to the ground he had first played on thirty-three years before and although his Norfolk side lost by 147 runs, he delighted the spectators with 36 runs and ended his innings with 22 scored off just six balls. Middlesex went out in the third round when Surrey won a high-scoring match by just 8 runs. Surrey made 280 for five and Middlesex replied with 272 for nine in a match decided by the fast bowling of Bob Willis who took six for 49.

FIRST CLASS RESULTS 1970
Championship Record

P	W	L	D	Pos
24	5	5	14	16th

April 20-30, **May** 1 beat Cambridge University by nine wickets at Fenners

May

2-5 drew with Hampshire at Lord's
6-8 drew with Glamorgan at Lord's
9-12 drew with Worcestershire at Lord's
16-19 beat Somerset by nine wickets at Taunton
20-2 drew with Northants at Northampton
23-6 drew with Sussex at Lord's
27-9 drew with Surrey at The Oval

June

10-11 beat Oxford University by 130 runs at The Parks
13-16 beat Nottinghamshire by 81 runs at Newark
17-19 lost to Lancashire by five wickets at Old Trafford
20-3 beat Gloucestershire by 103 runs at Bristol
27-30 drew with Derbyshire at Lord's

July

4-7 beat Kent by 136 runs at Lord's
11-14 drew with Essex at Westcliff
15-17 lost to Lancashire by ten wickets at Lord's
18-21 lost to Hampshire by four wickets at Basingstoke
25-8 drew with Northants at Lord's
29-31 beat Yorkshire by three wickets at Lord's

August

1-4 drew with Warwickshire at Lord's
5-7 drew with Kent at Canterbury
8-11 drew with Essex at Lord's
19-21 drew with Yorkshire at Scarborough
22-5 lost to Leicestershire by five wickets at Leicester
26-8 lost to Surrey by seven wickets at Lord's

August 29-31, **September** 1 drew with Sussex at Hove

Gillette Cup

April

28 beat Norfolk by 147 runs in first round at Lord's

May

30 beat Derbyshire by two wickets in second round at Lord's

July

8 lost to Surrey by 8 runs in the third round at The Oval

John Player League

April

26 lost to Lancashire by eight wickets at Old Trafford

May

10 match with Glamorgan at Lord's abandoned
17 lost to Somerset by two wickets at Bath

June

14 beat Nottinghamshire by 65 runs at Trent Bridge
21 beat Gloucestershire by 74 runs at Lydney
28 lost to Derbyshire by two wickets at Lord's

July

5 lost to Kent by five wickets at Lord's
12 lost to Essex by 43 runs at Westcliff
19 beat Hampshire by eight wickets at Portsmouth
26 lost to Northants by 39 runs at Lord's

August

2 lost to Warwickshire by four wickets at Lord's
9 beat Sussex by 60 runs at Lord's
16 beat Surrey by eight wickets at Lord's
23 lost to Leicestershire by 15 runs at Leicester
30 beat Worcestershire by 31 runs at Lord's

September

6 match with Yorkshire at Bradford abandoned

John Player League Record

P	W	L	NR	Pts	Pos
16	6	8	2	26	11th

1971

Brearley Steps Up

Mike Brearley assumed the captaincy of Middlesex in 1971 and guided the side to sixth place in the Championship, a position which would have been even better but for the fact that the county won only one game after 20 July, at which point they topped the table after beating Surrey at The Oval. Brearley had been tempted back to full-time cricket at Lord's with the offer of the captaincy, and Peter Parfitt stood down after leading the side for two full seasons. There were those who felt that Parfitt had been hard done by, but there was no doubt that the move significantly changed Middlesex's fortunes for the better. Under Brearley's leadership, individual members of the Middlesex team began to have a new belief in themselves and, just as he proved to be a great motivator of men at Test level later in his career, so Brearley carried Middlesex along with him in his first season as skipper.

It was a season of enterprising cricket and Middlesex supporters had seen precious little of that over the previous few years. At Lord's, eight out of twelve last-days of Championship matches saw run chases against the clock. In four of these Middlesex found themselves batting, and although they wasted commanding positions in three of these — against Notts, Glamorgan and Essex — there was still plenty of excitement to be had. Their bonus points tally shot up dramatically as well. Middlesex trebled the number of batting points which they achieved in the system's first season of 1968; and they took the club record number of points from one match on two occasions.

Four batsmen passed the 1,000 runs mark for the Championship season — Radley, Parfitt, Russell and Smith. Brearley and Featherstone missed the milestone by less than 100 runs each, and Parfitt and Russell each hit four centuries.

Peter Parfitt, relieved of the captaincy, passed his 1970 Championship aggregate quite comfortably and in looking back over his career with Middlesex to that point — a career which spanned some fifteen seasons — it is impossible to pinpoint any troughs. Eric Russell had made his four centuries — against Sussex,

Action man Peter Parfitt here hooking Robin Jackman of Surrey

Parfitt in the thick of the action again, though he and Radley missed this chance offered by Younis Ahmed 84

Glamorgan, Derbyshire and Leicestershire — by the middle of June.

Smith, Radley and Featherstone all scored less runs than in 1970, although it must be remembered that Mike Smith's unselfish search for batting bonus points often cost him personal glory. Even so, he did score two Championship centuries and gained the side several valuable points. Norman Featherstone enjoyed a good season with the ball and a late flourish saw him finish fifth in the national bowling averages. It was a spinner's summer, particularly at Lord's, and Fred Titmus took 100 wickets for the sixteenth time in his career — a feat bettered by only three bowlers in the entire history of cricket. Parfitt also took useful wickets as the side's third off-spinner, and Phil Edmonds captured fourteen wickets in five games. But the delight of the summer was Brearley's use of Latchman, who responded with eighteen wickets in his first two Championship games — one more than his entire 1970 haul — and went on to take seventy-seven at 25.98 each.

When Middlesex enjoyed a run of three consecutive victories — against Gloucestershire, Hampshire and Surrey in July, which took them to the top of the table — Latchman's leg-spinners accounted for twenty-two wickets in that spell. It said

> **Though Middlesex made the highest score of the game in their match with the Indians at Lord's in June 1971, they lost by two wickets. Scores: Middlesex 233 and 131; Indians 168 and 198 for eight. John Price took two wickets in two balls on each of the three days, also achieving that same feat on the Tuesday of the Pakistan Test on the same pitch.**

much for Brearley's brand of captaincy that he chose to use Latchman as a main bowler where other captains might have been too cautious to risk a leg-spinner in the changing climate of first-class cricket. Keith Jones made a rapid stride with seventy-one wickets at 21.80 each and John Price won back his Test place with one game against the Pakistanis and then played in all three Tests against India, although his county form in between the Tests brought him only forty-five wickets at 30.51.

Like most counties Middlesex suffered with the weather in 1971 and perhaps their most frustrating experience was at Neath in June where they were 290 runs ahead with one wicket to fall when heavy rain flooded the pitch on the third day. After making 213 in their first innings,

Middlesex bowled out Glamorgan for 178 on a wearing wicket, with Fred Titmus taking seven for 79 and Jones three for 30. When Eric Russell scored his fourth Cham-pionship century of the season with 116 in four hours, and he and Parfitt (56) put on 159 for the second wicket. It was a winning position until the rain came.

FIRST CLASS RESULTS 1971
Championship Record

P	W	L	D	Pos
24	7	6	11	6th

May
- 1-4 drew with Derbyshire at Derby
- 5-7 drew with Cambridge University at Fenners
- 8-11 drew with Nottinghamshire at Lord's
- 15-18 beat Leicestershire by ten wickets at Lord's
- 19-21 drew with Glamorgan at Lord's
- 26-8 lost to Yorkshire by eight wickets at Headingley

May 29-31, **June** 1 beat Sussex by 124 runs at Lord's

June
- 2-4 drew with Gloucestershire at Lord's
- 5-8 beat Northants by eight wickets at Lord's
- 9-11 drew with Worcestershire at Worcester
- 16-18 drew with Glamorgan at Neath
- 23-5 lost to India by two wickets at Lord's
- 26-9 lost to Kent by five wickets at Lord's

July
- 3-6 drew with Yorkshire at Lord's
- 10-13 beat Gloucestershire by five wickets at Gloucester
- 14-16 beat Hampshire by four wickets at Lord's
- 17-20 beat Surrey by 118 runs at The Oval
- 21-3 lost to Nottinghamshire by 192 runs at Worksop

July 31, **August** 2-3 drew with Kent at Canterbury

August
- 4-6 drew with Essex at Lord's
- 7-10 drew with Warwickshire at Coventry
- 11-13 drew with Lancashire at Blackpool
- 14-17 lost to Surrey by five wickets at Lord's
- 18-20 lost to Somerset by 98 runs at Taunton
- 25-7 beat Somerset by nine wickets at Lord's
- 28-31 lost to Sussex by one wicket at Hove

Gillette Cup

June
- 12 lost to Surrey by 29 runs in the second round at The Oval

John Player League

May
- 2 lost to Worcestershire by eight wickets at Worcester
- 16 beat Yorkshire by 27 runs at Lord's
- 23 beat Glamorgan by 9 runs at Ebbw Vale
- 30 lost to Somerset by seven wickets at Lord's

June
- 6 beat Lancashire by 31 runs at Lord's
- 20 lost to Warwickshire by one wicket at Edgbaston
- 27 lost to Essex by 36 runs at Lord's

July
- 4 lost to Hampshire by 27 runs at Lord's
- 18 lost to Sussex by 130 runs at Hove
- 25 beat Surrey by 124 runs at The Oval

August
- 1 lost to Leicestershire by 22 runs at Lord's
- 8 lost to Northamptonshire by nine wickets at Wellingborough
- 15 lost to Derbyshire by 5 runs at Derby
- 22 beat Gloucestershire by faster scoring rate at Lord's
- 29 beat Nottinghamshire by 29 runs at Lord's

September
- 12 lost to Kent by 38 runs at Canterbury

John Player League Record

P	W	L	NR	Pts	Pos
16	6	10	0	24	13th

1972
Promises Unfulfilled

On 12 June 1972 Middlesex cricket was riding high. It was the second day of the Hampshire match at Lord's where Middlesex were 106 ahead on first innings and looked certain to win the game and better their position of fourth in the Championship. The previous day they had beaten Kent by one run in the John Player League match at Folkestone, a victory which saw them head the JPL table; they were through to the quarter-finals of the new Benson and Hedges 55-over knockout competition, and were due to meet Gloucestershire two days later; and the draw for the Gillette Cup had paired them with Essex, who they had already beaten twice that season in one-day competitions. All in all, Middlesex cricket was in a splendid position on which to build and take one or more honours after years in the wilderness.

On the first day of the Hampshire match Middlesex had made 296 with all but Mike Smith contributing useful runs. When Hampshire batted they were always struggling against a tight Middlesex attack and Jones led the wicket-takers

with six victims as the visitors wobbled to 190 all out. When Middlesex batted again on the evening of the second day they collapsed to 31 for six in the face of some accurate bowling from Bob Herman, who captured the wickets of his former teammates Smith, Parfitt, Brearley and Murray. On the last day the Middlesex innings was wrapped up at 86 all out (Herman five for 47) and Hampshire had little difficulty in reaching 193 for five and victory. It was a remarkable turnaround in Middlesex's fortunes after their commanding position on the second day.

That match against Hampshire not only signalled the end of Middlesex's hopes for the 1972 Championship, it also marked the beginning of a spell in which the club would lose any chances of honours in the one-day competitions that season. On the Wednesday following the Lord's defeat, Middlesex went down to Gloucestershire by 62 runs in the Benson and Hedges quarter-finals. Gloucestershire batted first and made 238 for nine. After Nicholls had been caught by Smith off Mike Selvey with only two runs on the board, Sadiq and Knight added 90 for the second wicket, followed by a stand of 108 in only sixteen overs between Knight and Procter. Middlesex, apart from brief flashes, never got to grips with the scoring rate required to bring them to victory and dreams of a Lord's final evaporated.

Although Middlesex had beaten Essex in the John Player League and the Benson and Hedges Cup already that season, there was no hat-trick of victories in the Gillette Cup. On a controversial Westcliff pitch, Keith Boyce and John Lever each took five wickets as Middlesex were shot out for 41 in less than twenty overs. Only John Murray reached double figures and with Price out through injury, Middlesex could do little to stop Essex cruising home

Mike Brearley drives Geoff Arnold during the Benson and Hedges Cup group match at The Oval

with eight wickets to spare. This just left the John Player League for Middlesex but, after a run of four successive wins in July and early August, they fell at the final hurdles, losing their last three games at Eastbourne, Lord's and Trent Bridge. Parfitt was left out for the game against Warwickshire when Middlesex lost by just one run, and a five-run defeat at Trent Bridge saw them end their season, once full of hope, empty-handed.

Middlesex finished eighth in the Championship, the season marking the retirement of Eric Russell and Peter Parfitt,

Middlesex qualified for the Benson and Hedges quarter finals in the 1972 South Group.					
	P	W	L	Bwlg	Pts
Middlesex	4	3	1	1	10
Sussex	4	3	1	1	10
Kent	4	2	2	2	8
Surrey	4	2	2	1	7
Essex	4	0	4	0	0

although Parfitt was playing well enough to appear in the last three Test Matches of the summer against Australia when he distinguished himself at Trent Bridge with 46 vital runs to save England's face. Parfitt scored only 947 Championship runs, but he headed the averages with 41.17 and scored three centuries, one of which came in his last first-class appearance at Lord's, when his 129 helped Middlesex to an innings win over Derbyshire. Sadly, Russell did not make a century in his last season — his highest score was 99 against Nottinghamshire — and he was dropped for the last four games. Only Radley and Smith passed the 1,000 runs, although remember the Championship was now down to just twenty matches for each team. Radley, in particular, looked an accomplished batsman and many felt he was unlucky not to go to India and Pakistan with MCC in 1972-3.

Mike Smith was one of only two Middlesex players to pass 1,000 Championship runs in 1972

John Price headed the bowling averages with sixty-five wickets at 19.89 each and Keith Jones came second with forty-one at 28.34 apiece. The pace attack was strengthened by the inclusion of Mike Selvey who played in nineteen games and took forty-five wickets at 32.51. Edmonds had fourteen at 28.71, Titmus fifty-two at 31.92 and Latchman twenty-seven at 38.40. Price was back to his devastating best in many matches and Selvey shared the new ball with him, leaving Jones to come on as third change. Two Middlesex players went on and on. Fred Titmus celebrated his twenty-fourth season and John Murray was there as always, immaculate behind the stumps.

FIRST CLASS RESULTS 1972
Championship Record

P	W	L	D	Pos
20	5	5	10	8th

May

3-5   drew with Leicestershire at Lord's

6-9   drew with Oxford University at The Parks

10-12   drew with Somerset at Taunton

24-6   drew with Nottinghamshire at Lord's

27-30   beat Sussex by nine wickets at Lord's

May 31, **June** 1-2, drew with Worcestershire at Kidderminster

June

7-9   drew with Yorkshire at Lord's

10-13   lost to Hampshire by five wickets at Lord's

17-20   lost to Warwickshire by ten wickets at Edgbaston

July

1-4   drew with Surrey at The Oval

5-7   lost to Kent by seven wickets at Maidstone

8-11   lost to the Australians by five wickets at Lord's

12-14   drew with Essex at Westcliff

15-18   beat Lancashire by seven wickets at Lord's

July 29-31, **August** 1 drew with Kent at Lord's

August

5-8   drew with Surrey at Lord's

9-10   lost to Northants by innings and 65 runs at Lord's

12-15   beat Gloucestershire by six wickets at Cheltenham

19-22   beat Derbyshire by innings and 61 runs at Lord's

23-5   lost to Yorkshire by 98 runs at Headingley

26-9   beat Sussex by three wickets at Hove

August 30-1, **September** 1 drew with Glamorgan at Cardiff

Gillette Cup

July

19   lost to Essex by eight wickets in the second round at Westcliff

John Player League

April

30   beat Gloucestershire by eight wickets at Lord's

May

7   beat Northants by 35 runs at Northampton

21   beat Essex by 68 runs at Lord's

June

4   match with Hampshire abandoned at Lord's

11   beat Kent by one run at Folkestone

18   match with Derbyshire abandoned at Buxton

25   lost to Surrey by 3 runs at Byfleet

July

2   lost to Leicestershire by 19 runs at Lord's

9   lost to Yorkshire by 13 runs at Lord's

16   beat Glamorgan by 7 runs at Cardiff

23   beat Lancashire by nine wickets at Old Trafford

30   beat Somerset by five wickets at Lord's

August

6   beat Worcestershire by faster scoring rate at Lord's

13   lost to Sussex by 29 runs at Eastbourne

20   lost to Warwickshire by 1 run at Lord's

September

3   lost to Nottinghamshire by 5 runs at Trent Bridge

John Player League Record

P	W	L	NR	Pts	Pos
16	8	6	2	34	5th

Benson and Hedges Cup
South Section

April 29, **May** 1 beat Kent by three wickets at Lord's

May

13-15   lost to Sussex by 47 runs at Hove

20-2   beat Surrey by 13 runs at The Oval

June

3-5   beat Essex by 51 runs at Lord's

14   lost to Gloucestershire by 62 runs in the quarter-finals at Lord's

1973

A Strange Affair

The Middlesex campaign of 1973 was a strange affair. By the middle of July their first twelve games in the Championship had failed to produce a win and they had lost four times, four of the remaining eight draws being curtailed by the weather. The Benson and Hedges qualifying matches had seen them win only once and finish bottom of the zonal table. Yet in the John Player League, Middlesex had won six out of their first nine games, including five on the trot after the first match of the season against Kent at Maidstone was abandoned. It seemed that success in the JPL looked assured; and that the Championship would see Middlesex struggling in the lower reaches of the table. Yet there was to be a transformation. On 17 July, Middlesex completed a fine ten-wickets win over Kent at Dover and after that lost only one more Championship game and enjoyed three wins and a tied match. In the John Player League, Middlesex lost five of their last seven games, won only one, and had another abandoned. The result of this turnabout was that Middlesex finished eighth in the JPL and thirteenth in the Championship.

Looking at the statistics of this Middlesex season it is plain to see that the lack of top-class penetrative bowlers caused many of the side's problems in the three-day games, for when Phil Edmonds came into the side after the Cambridge University season, and John Price, who had gone into semi-retirement, also came back at the same time, Middlesex looked a different side. Both Edmonds and Price returned for the win at Dover in mid-July and the pair went on to head the Middlesex bowling averages with almost identical figures.

Price had given some idea of how much Middlesex would miss him when he played in the game against Sussex at Lord's in May and took four for 36 in the first innings. When he returned for the end of the season he helped Mike Selvey, operating at the other end, to look a better bowler. Selvey was gaining a reputation on the county cricket circuit as a bowler who could move the ball through the air and off seam and his stamina was quite phenomenal. Edmonds had taken twenty-nine first-class wickets for Cambridge and his arrival at Lord's signalled the end of Harry Latchman's Middlesex career. Leg spinners were now a luxury and here was Edmonds, a left-armer, who could turn the ball away from the bat with a finger spin, whereas Latchman achieved the same, but with the less predictable wrist spin which was becoming obsolete. The demise of the leg-spinner is a regretable feature of modern cricket. Fred Titmus took thirty of his seventy-two Championship wickets in August and the season's haul took him past J. T. Hearne's record aggregate of 2,093 wickets for Middlesex, and to wider glory as only the fourth player in history — behind W. G. Grace, George Hirst and Wilfred Rhodes — to reach 20,000 runs and 2,500 wickets in first-class cricket.

Gomes is bowled by Simmons of Lancashire in the Gillette Cup quarter-final match at Lord's

The retirement of Russell and Parfitt obviously found Middlesex's batting line-up somewhat weaker and Mike Smith was the only man to pass 1,000, topping the averages at 49.96 per innings. The Championship, of course, now consisted of only twenty matches and the days of several batsmen from each county passing 1,000 runs was a thing of the past. Radley's form slipped but, after an indecisive start, Featherstone picked up to score five 50s in his first eight games. Brearley moved up the order and played well; and John Murray scored his first century for Middlesex since 1969. In fact, he made two consecutive hundreds.

Middlesex's Championship revival began at Dover when Kent were bowled out for 173. John Price, returning to the side, took six for 27 in that innings when the Dover wicket was of uneven bounce. The Kent innings folded after lunch when they went from 110 for two to 173 all out with Price enjoying a spell of five wickets for five runs in seven overs. John Shepherd troubled Middlesex when they batted but Brearley (82), Smith (76) and Featherstone (57) guided them to a lead of 104. Kent looked like making a better fight of their second innings, getting to within five runs of avoiding the innings defeat with only two wickets down. Then Denness retired hurt, four wickets fell for 12 runs, Selvey finished with five for 59 and Smith (45) and Featherstone (51) had no difficulty in steering Middlesex to a ten-wickets win.

In the last game of the season Middlesex tied with Yorkshire. It was the first such Championship result since Middlesex and Hampshire tied in 1967 and only the second time that Yorkshire had shared the honours so equally, the first time being against Leicestershire at Huddersfield in 1954. Middlesex were bowled out for 102 (Nicholson five for 23) and Yorkshire declared their innings closed at 106 for nine after nineteen wickets fell on the first day. Brearley's 83 enabled Middlesex to reach 211 all out in their second innings, leaving Yorkshire 208 to win with plenty of time. At the close of the second day Yorkshire were 121 for three but wickets continued to fall and those Yorkshire players who were suffering from a virus were called upon to bat. Selvey took six for 74 and it was fitting that he should end the game by clean bowling Robinson with the scores level.

Featherstone pulls Geoff Arnold for 4 at Lord's

Top of the Middlesex Championship bowling averages in 1973, Edmonds and Price had almost identical figures.				
	O	M	R	W	Ave
Edmonds	238.5	88	535	30	17.8
Price	185.1	43	466	26	17.9

FIRST CLASS RESULTS 1973
Championship Record

P	W	L	D	Tied	Pos
20	4	5	10	1	13th

May
- 2-4 drew with Gloucestershire at Lord's
- 9-11 lost to Somerset by innings and 11 runs at Lord's
- 16-18 drew with Lancashire at Old Trafford
- 19-22 drew with Nottinghamshire at Trent Bridge
- 23-5 lost to Essex by seven wickets at Lord's
- 26-9 drew with Sussex at Lord's

June
- 6-8 lost to Kent by eight wickets at Lord's
- 9-12 drew with Glamorgan at Lord's
- 16-18 lost to Northants by innings and 127 runs at Lord's
- 23-6 drew with Derbyshire at Burton-upon-Trent

June 30, **July** 2-3 drew with Worcestershire at Lord's

July
- 4-6 drew with the West Indians at Lord's
- 7-10 drew with Leicestershire at Leicester
- 14-17 beat Kent by ten wickets at Dover
- 18-20 drew with Hampshire at Basingstoke

August
- 4-7 drew with Surrey at Lord's
- 8-10 beat Warwickshire by eight wickets at Lord's
- 11-14 beat Yorkshire by innings and 46 runs at Lord's
- 18-21 lost to Surrey by 29 runs at The Oval
- 25-8 beat Sussex by 182 runs at Hove

September
- 8-11 tied with Yorkshire at Bradford

Gillette Cup

July
- 11 beat Nottinghamshire by four wickets in the second round at Lord's

August
- 1-2 beat Lancashire by four wickets in the third round at Lord's
- 15 lost to Sussex by 5 runs in the semi-final at Lord's

John Player League

May
- 6 match with Kent abandoned at Maidstone
- 13 beat Sussex by five wickets at Lord's
- 20 beat Lancashire by 17 runs at Old Trafford
- 27 beat Nottinghamshire by 66 runs at Trent Bridge

June
- 3 beat Somerset by 6 runs at Lord's
- 17 beat Northants by two wickets at Lord's
- 24 lost to Derbyshire by one run at Chesterfield

July
- 1 beat Worcestershire by four wickets at Lord's
- 8 lost to Warwickshire by 21 runs at Lord's
- 15 lost to Essex by 17 runs at Westcliff
- 22 lost to Gloucestershire by 65 runs at Lydney
- 29 beat Leicestershire by 13 runs at Lord's

August
- 5 match with Surrey at The Oval abandoned
- 12 lost to Yorkshire by 19 runs at Lord's
- 19 lost to Hampshire by five wickets at Lord's

September
- 2 lost to Glamorgan by 41 runs at Swansea

John Player League Record

P	W	L	T	NR	Pts	Pos
16	7	7	0	2	30	7th=

Benson and Hedges Cup
South Group

April
- 28 lost to Kent by 45 runs at Canterbury

May
- 7-8 beat Surrey by 5 runs at Lord's
- 12 lost to Sussex by eight wickets at Lord's

June
- 2 lost to Essex by ten wickets at Harlow

1974

Spin Twins

Freddie Titmus and Phil Edmonds revelled during 1974 when Middlesex finished sixth in the Championship, thanks to some fine bowling by the 'spin twins'. Titmus and Edmonds together accounted for 156 wickets while the rest of the Middlesex bowlers could amass only 116 between them. Certainly the pitches helped both men and they took full advantage. Titmus bowled so well that, at the age of forty-one, he was selected to tour Australia with MCC, six years after the accident in the West Indies which threatened to end his career altogether. Just as Selvey had benefited from Price's presence the previous season, so Edmonds found that bowling in partnership with Titmus helped him to establish a secure place in the Middlesex team.

Middlesex's final position of sixth was a disappointment if one considers that with three weeks remaining of the season, they were fifth in the table with four successive victories under their belts. Wins over Glamorgan, Yorkshire, Kent and Surrey set them up for a final run-in over the last three games which, if negotiated successfully, could lift them to honours for the first time since 1949. But the next game, at Hove, was the beginning of another slide. Clive Radley made a fine 106 not out in a respectable Middlesex first innings total of 294. But Sussex found batting even easier and thanks to Greenidge (133) and Graves (104 not out) they were able to declare at 336 for four. Middlesex's second innings wilted out before Snow and Phillipson and they were all out for 196, leaving Sussex to score 155 which they did in less than two hours. Mark Faber reached his century with a 6 and was 112 not out when the winning run was struck.

This defeat was followed by an even more disasterous match at Lord's where the pitch was declared unfit by both Brearley and Ray Illingworth, as well as umpires Crapp and Rhodes. Leicestershire batted first and made 269 with Brian Davison's 109 containing one 6 and fifteen 4s. John Murray was the highest scorer in Middlesex's reply of 204 when he made 47 before falling to the Australian McKenzie. Edmonds added five second innings wickets to the four he claimed earlier, and Leicestershire struggled to 214, leaving Middlesex to score an impossible 280 for victory on a pitch which had seen even the spinners lift the ball head-high. Middlesex had no answer to McKenzie and McVicker. The Leicestershire pair bowled

The great Sobers is bowled by Jones after scoring 74 for Notts at Lord's

unchanged and after nineteen overs Middlesex were all out for 41. It was Leicestershire's first Championship win at Lord's. McVicker finished with six for 19, and McKenzie four for 22.

The last game of the season — against Northants, also at Lord's — started the following day and soon there was another procession of Middlesex batsmen on their

> **Mike Brearley scored an unbeaten 173 against Glamorgan at Cardiff and followed it up two days later with 163 not out against Yorkshire at Lord's.**

way to the pavilion. They stood at 36 for six (the previous day they had fallen to an amazing 10 for six) before Edmonds and Titmus pulled the innings together. Edmonds was particularly severe on Bedi and made 57 before the Indian spinner finally had him caught by Tait. Middlesex totalled 144 and Northants had made 55 for the loss of Tait when the rain came down and wiped out the last two day's play. The season was at an end and yet again Middlesex had failed to win a major honour although it should be recorded that the under-25 side took their title for the third successive year and the second eleven won the Second XI Championship.

Apart from the obvious successes of Titmus and Edmonds, Middlesex's bowling struggled in 1974. Price topped the averages after coming back to the side in July, but he lacked a penetrative partner. Mike Selvey, after his promise of the previous season, was dropped for a spell. He had started with a good match against Hampshire when he took nine wickets, including the scalp of Barry Richards twice, and when he came back into the side he took six wickets against Surrey, although they cost him 109 runs — a measure of how expensive he proved this season. Keith Jones did so badly that Middlesex released him at the end of the season, and of the two youngsters tried in his place — Lamb and Vernon — it was

Vernon who looked the more promising, taking eleven wickets in only his third game. The Honourable Timothy Lamb, an Oxford Blue, managed only five wickets for 270 runs in his ninety-four overs.

Three players reached 1,000 Championship runs — Brearley, Smith and Radley to put them in their order at the top of the Middlesex batting averages. Radley scored three hundreds, Brearley, Featherstone, and Smith two each, with Brearley's unbeaten 173 against Glamorgan at Cardiff, the highest of any of them. Smith made 170 against Kent at Canterbury and also scored a century for Middlesex against the Pakistanis at Lord's to add to his two Championship hundreds. Featherstone averaged 30 with 891 runs but Middlesex lacked the extra batsman who would have made all the difference to their chances of winning run-chases or

Murray and Radley miss a chance offered by Derek Randall in the same match. Unlucky bowler was Mike Selvey

setting up formidable targets. There was hope for Larry Gomes, especially after his good season with Trinidad in the Shell Shield, but it was another West Indian youngster, Barbadian Roland Butcher, who looked the best prospect in his five games in which he averaged 21.42.

FIRST CLASS RESULTS 1974
Championship Record

P	W	L	D	Pos
20	7	5	8	6th

May
1-3   beat Hampshire by 100 runs at Lord's
8-10   lost to Warwickshire by ten wickets at Edgbaston
15-17   drew with Nottinghamshire at Lord's
22-4   drew with Gloucestershire at Bristol
25-8   drew with Sussex at Lord's

June
5-7   lost to Lancashire by eight wickets at Lord's
8-11   beat Derbyshire by eight wickets at Lord's
15-18   drew with Essex at Ilford
22-4   beat Yorkshire by eight wickets at Middlesbrough

July
1-2   lost to the Pakistanis by six wickets at Lord's
3-5   drew with Kent at Lord's
6-9   drew with Surrey at The Oval
13-16   lost to Somerset by 73 runs at Taunton
17-19   drew with Worcestershire at Worcester
24-6   beat Glamorgan by nine wickets at Cardiff
27-30   beat Yorkshire by 104 runs at Lord's

August
3-6   beat Kent by innings and 63 runs at Canterbury
17-20   beat Surrey by ten wickets at Lord's
24-7   lost to Sussex by nine wickets at Hove
28-30   lost to Leicestershire by 238 runs at Lord's
August 31, **September** 2-3   drew with Northants at Lord's

Gillette Cup

July
10-11   lost to Lancashire by 81 runs in the second round at Lord's

John Player League

May
5   lost to Worcestershire by 60 runs at Worcester
12   lost to Hampshire by one wicket at Southampton
19   lost to Warwickshire by 13 runs at Edgbaston
26   beat Sussex by 37 runs at Hove

June
2   beat Glamorgan by four wickets at Lord's
9   beat Northants by 26 runs at Tring
16   lost to Surrey by five wickets at Lord's
23   lost to Yorkshire by 125 runs at Headingley
30   tied with Lancashire at Lord's

July
7   beat Gloucestershire by 29 runs at Lord's
14   lost to Somerset by 16 runs at Taunton
28   beat Essex by six wickets at Lord's

August
4   match with Kent abandoned at Lord's
11   lost to Leicestershire by seven wickets at Leicester
18   beat Nottinghamshire on faster scoring rate at Lord's
25   beat Derbyshire by seven wickets at Lord's

John Player League Record

P	W	L	T	NR	Pts	Pos
16	7	7	1	1	32	8th

Benson and Hedges Cup
Midland Selection

April
27   lost to Warwickshire by six wickets at Coventry

May
4   lost to Northants by three wickets at Lord's
18   lost to Leicestershire by 5 runs at Leicester

June
1   lost to Worcestershire by 57 runs at Lord's

1975

Double Runners-Up

For Middlesex, 1975 was a season more noted for success in the limited-overs competitions than the first-class game. They reached the finals of both the Gillette and Benson and Hedges Cups, although having got that far, the side then capitulated to Lancashire and Leicestershire respectively. Middlesex's progress in the limited-overs game was achieved without the help of really penetrative seam bowling and although this shortcoming was overcome in the two cups, it was painfully apparent in the Championship. The first win did not come until Hampshire were beaten in June, and although a victory at Scarborough quickly followed, Middlesex then had to wait for another six games for their next win. This started a run of three successive victories — including a win over Kent in Kent for the third year running — and then Warwickshire became Middlesex's last victims, losing to the county for the fourth time in all competitions in 1975.

The pace attack struggled all summer with John Price taking ten wickets at 23.20 in just four games. Selvey bagged sixty-four at 28.78 each, Tim Lamb having thirty-seven at 29.91. Vernon, after looking the more promising in 1974, disappeared among the 'also bowled' with two wickets for 229 runs. Off-spinner John Emburey played in four games and took fifteen wickets at 19.06 to top the averages, Edmonds had sixty-five at 24.53, and Titmus, struggling after a good winter tour, fifty-seven at 30.92. Edmonds won his England debut in the Third Test and started sensationally with three wickets in fifteen balls. He finished with five for 28 against Australia in the famous Test at Headingley where the pitch was dug up and the match abandoned.

John Murray retired at the end of the season after passing Herbert Strudwick's two records with 1,270 catches and 1,527 dismissals altogether. Murray had played twenty-four seasons for Middlesex and his

> Middlesex were bowled out for 59 against Gloucestershire at Lord's in July 1975 and at one stage had reached 12 runs for seven wickets. Despite making 379 when asked to follow-on, Middlesex lost by three wickets.

immaculate wicketkeeping, coupled with batting of the highest calibre at county level, puts him among the truly great cricketers to have represented Middlesex. In the county's batting, fourteen centuries were scored with Mike Brearley leading the way with eight, Murray and Radley each scoring five. Brearley led the averages with 1,656 runs at 53.41, and Radley, Featherstone and Smith joined him on 1,000 runs for the season. Brearley had a fine season in a summer which, despite giving us a scorching cricket season after the beginning of June, was not noted for the reliability of its pitches. He ended the campaign as the second-highest Englishman in the national averages and in

Congratulations! 31 May 1975 and John Murray has just passed Herbert Strudwick's world record of wicketkeeping dismissals. A catch to dismiss Surrey's Owen Thomas off the bowling of Tim Lamb gave Murray 1,494 victims

Glamorgan's John Hopkins turns to see Clive Radley take a smart slip catch to dismiss him without scoring at Lord's

the Benson and Hedges competition quietly with a defeat at the hands of Essex at Lord's and after Featherstone took the Gold Award with 56 vital runs in the defeat of Sussex, Middlesex lost to Kent by 2 runs. They needed 8 off the last over but failed. Earlier, Kent's John Shepherd had scored a wondrous 96 after Kent were struggling at 53 for eight. Edmonds took four for 11 but it was Shepherd who deservedly had the Gold Award.

Middlesex now needed to beat the Minor Counties South to qualify but the amateurs made them fight all the way, only yielding their last wicket — which Middlesex had to capture to overtake Sussex's striking rate — in the last over when Barlow ran out Yeabsley. Even then Middlesex were made to struggle in passing Minor Counties' 168, which they did with two wickets and four balls to spare. A fine all-round team performance saw them beat Yorkshire with five balls to spare in the quarter-final; and in keeping with these nail-biting finishes, Middlesex went into the final after a victory over Warwickshire, Price taking three wickets in his last two overs to leave Warwickshire 3 runs adrift at the end of their overs. It was Warwickshire who were beaten in the second round of the Gillette Cup, three days before Middlesex met Leicestershire in the Benson and Hedges final at Lord's.

Edmonds opened the final innings with Smith and hooked the second ball of the match for 6, but it was not a sign of things to come. Only Smith's painstaking 83 steered Middlesex to an all out score of 146. Although Leicestershire made a slow start, they never looked like failing to score a victory and their winning run came with only five men out and twenty-two balls still unused. In the Gillette Cup final, Middlesex again batted first on a dampish pitch and were 180 for eight when their overs ran out. Although Murray crowned his last Middlesex appearance with a brilliant one-handed catch to get rid of Hayes, Clive Lloyd was dropped by Smith at mid-on and the big West Indian went on to score an unbeaten 73 as Lancashire got home with three overs and seven wickets to spare.

seventh place overall. For the other leading batsman it was a summer of mixed fortunes. Both Smith and Radley scored more runs than in 1974, but Smith's average went down from 42.57 to 33.63. Featherstone produced flashes of brilliance — including two superb undefeated hundreds in the defeat of Kent at Canterbury — but Roland Butcher and Graham Barlow both failed to impress consistently.

It was the one-day cups which brought the Middlesex season to life. They started

P	W	L	D	Pos
20	6	7	7	11th

April 30, **May** 1-2 drew with Kent at Lord's
May
14-16   drew with Somerset at Lord's
24-7   lost to Sussex by 188 runs at Hove
28-30   lost to Essex by three wickets at Lord's
May 31, **June** 2-3 drew with Surrey at Lord's
June
7-10   beat Hampshire by 135 runs at Southampton
14-17   beat Yorkshire by 20 runs at Scarborough
18-20   lost to Lancashire by eight wickets at Old Trafford
June 28-30, **July** 1 drew with Worcestershire at Lord's
July
5-8   drew with Nottinghamshire at Trent Bridge
9-11   lost to Gloucestershire by three wickets at Lord's
12-15   drew with Surrey at The Oval
26-9   beat Northants by five wickets at Northampton
August
2-5   beat Kent by 156 runs at Canterbury
9-11   beat Glamorgan by ten wickets at Lord's
13-15   lost to Yorkshire by 5 runs at Lord's
23-6   lost to Sussex by eight wickets at Lord's
27-9   beat Warwickshire by 111 runs at Lord's
August 30, **September** 1-2, drew with Derbyshire at Chesterfield
September
3-5   lost to Leicestershire by eight wickets at Leicester

Gillette Cup

June
25   beat Buckinghamshire by 99 runs in the first round at Lord's
July
16   beat Warwickshire by 127 runs in the second round at Edgbaston
August
6   beat Worcestershire by eight wickets in the third round at Worcester
20   beat Derbyshire by 24 runs in the semi-final at Chesterfield
September
6   lost to Lancashire by seven wickets in the final at Lord's

John Player League

May
4   beat Northants by 18 runs at Lord's
11   lost to Kent by eight wickets at Folkestone
18   lost to Derbyshire by five wickets at Chesterfield
25   lost to Hampshire by 56 runs at Lord's
June
8   beat Gloucestershire by 59 runs at Bristol
22   lost to Surrey by 18 runs at The Oval
29   lost to Worcestershire by seven wickets at Lord's
July
6   beat Leicestershire by 27 runs at Lord's
13   lost to Essex by 6 runs at Chelmsford
20   lost to Nottinghamshire by 24 runs at Trent Bridge
27   lost to Yorkshire by ten wickets at Lord's
August
10   lost to Somerset by nine wickets at Lord's
17   lost to Lancashire by five wickets at Old Trafford
24   beat Warwickshire by 9 runs at Lord's
31   beat Sussex by 37 runs at Lord's
September
14   beat Glamorgan by 98 runs at Cardiff

John Player League Record

P	W	L	T	NR	Pts	Pos
16	7	9	0	0	28	10th

Benson and Hedges Cup
South Section

April
26   lost to Essex by 82 runs at Lord's
May
5   beat Sussex by five wickets at Hove
17-19   lost to Kent by 2 runs at Lord's
21   beat Minor Counties (South) by two wickets at Amersham
June
4   beat Yorkshire by four wickets in quarter-final at Lord's
July
2   beat Warwickshire by 3 runs in the semi-final at Edgbaston
19   lost to Leicestershire by five wickets in final at Lord's

1976
Champions!

Middlesex were champions! In the long hot summer of 1976 the county took their first outright hold on the Championship since the equally golden summer of 1947 when Denis Compton and Bill Edrich held sway. Now a new breed of Middlesex cricketer had brought honour back to Lord's after so many years of indifferent performances had frustrated supporters of the club. Yet there was no hint of the glory to come at the start of the season when after beating Kent, Middlesex lost to Warwickshire and drew with Northants and Surrey to net only thirty-two points from the first four games. But then followed a run of four consecutive victories — against Essex, Sussex, Somerset and, most significantly Gloucestershire who finished third. The win over Gloucestershire was completed in only eleven hours of play after Selvey took seven wickets when they were bowled out for only 55 to

John Steele's middle stump is uprooted by Mike Gatting on the first day of the Championship match with Leicestershire at Lord's

set Middlesex up for an innings win.

Middlesex's next six games saw them lose four times. But with victories over Sussex and Nottinghamshire in the other two of those games, and the steady amassing of bonus points, the defeats were not critical and when Nottinghamshire were beaten by four wickets at Lord's on 27 July, Middlesex went to the top of the table and stayed there. Defeat by Kent at Dartford — after Kent had been asked to follow-on — was quickly put behind Middlesex and was followed by a morale-boosting win over the West Indians to give Middlesex the honour of becoming the only county to beat the tourists in 1976.

Three more wins quickly followed when Derbyshire, Essex and Glamorgan were each beaten handsomely, although Essex did push them a little harder than the other two counties, neither of whom had the answer to the Middlesex spin attack. When Lancashire gave up their run-chase at Lord's and batted out time, there was some anxiety which was heightened in the next match at Worcester when rain spoiled any chance of a result. This now left Middlesex to play their old rivals Surrey at The Oval while Gloucestershire met Derbyshire. Gloucestershire lost to Derbyshire at Bristol, but it was all rather academic, for Middlesex also triumphed at The Oval. There was no need for pocket calculators — Middlesex took the title with points to spare. John Edrich scored the ninety-ninth century of his first class career to hold up Middlesex but they eventually took the game by five wickets, having already clocked up enough bonus points to secure the title by 4pm on the second day.

There is no doubt that the Middlesex spinners played a major role in the title win. It was a summer of bone-hard worn pitches, and Titmus, Edmonds and Featherstone reaped a rich harvest of wickets. Featherstone's thirty-two victims at 14.75 each not only put him on top of the Middlesex averages, they also helped him to be-

Clive Radley takes runs off Hampshire's Taylor at Lord's

come the first Middlesex player to head the national bowling averages since G.O.Allen in 1935. Titmus had sixty-five at 21.66 and Edmonds sixty-four at 25.57 apiece. But there were other bowling successes too. Somerset's Jones came to take a lion's share of the pace bowling with sixty-nine wickets, and Selvey had sixty-one, while Lamb finished second in the averages with nineteen at 17.89

The batting saw three players top 1,000 runs and the revelation of the summer was Graham Barlow who scored three centuries, including an undefeated 160 against Derbyshire at Lord's, and made 1,282 Championship runs to head the averages with 49.30. Barlow's other centuries were 140 not out at Chelmsford and 132 at Hove, and he, above all the other Middlesex successes, was the outstanding batsman of the season. Brearley and Smith both topped 1,000 runs and Fea-

---

When Middlesex took the Championship at The Oval, three members of their 1947 title-winning side were present. W. J. Edrich, F. T. Mann and H. P. Sharp saw this latest triumph.

therstone and Radley were the other main batsmen, although Radley had the misfortune to break a finger. He came back well, however, with centuries at Chelmsford and Swansea.

It should be remembered that this splendid Championship victory was achieved at a time when crucial players were often missing. Brearley and Selvey played in the Test series against the West Indians, Barlow was picked for England in the one-day Prudential matches, and youngsters Gatting and Gould went on the Young England tour to the West Indies in the second half of the season. Add to that several injuries to other players and the Middlesex achievement is even more worthy. Even before the start of the season Middlesex had lost Gomes who disappeared from the county scene. The one-day competitions brought Middlesex no successes — but with the Championship now at Lord's that could be forgiven.

FIRST CLASS RESULTS 1976
Championship Record

P	W	L	D	Pos
20	11	5	4	1st

April
24-7 beat Oxford University by six wickets at The Parks
28-30 beat Kent by 97 runs at Lord's
May
5-7 drew with Northants at Lord's
12-14 lost to Warwickshire by eight wickets at Edgbaston
19-21 beat Cambridge University by ten wickets at Fenners
May 29-31, **June** 1 drew with Surrey at Lord's
June
2-4 beat Essex by six wickets at Lord's
5-7 beat Sussex by nine wickets at Hove
12-13 beat Somerset by innings and 47 runs at Bath
16-18 beat Gloucestershire by innings and 115 runs at Gloucester
26-9 lost to Hampshire by six wickets at Lord's
July
7-9 beat Sussex by innings and 54 runs at Lord's
10-13 lost to Yorkshire by 1 run at Bradford
21-3 lost to Leicestershire by 301 runs at Lord's
24-7 beat Nottinghamshire by four wickets at Lord's
28-30 lost to Kent by 57 runs at Dartford
July 31, **August** 2-3 beat the West Indians by four wickets at Lord's
August
7-10 beat Derbyshire by 106 runs at Lord's
11-13 beat Essex by 36 runs at Chelmsford
14-17 beat Glamorgan by 168 runs at Swansea
25-7 drew with Lancashire at Lord's
28-31 drew with Worcestershire at Worcester
September
1-3 beat Surrey by five wickets at The Oval

Gillette Cup

July
14 lost to Lancashire by three wickets in the second round at Old Trafford

John Player League

April
25 lost to Sussex by 36 runs at Hove
May
2 beat Kent by 48 runs at Lord's
16 beat Gloucestershire by five wickets at Lord's
23 lost to Hampshire by 18 runs at Basingstoke
30 beat Nottinghamshire by six wickets at Lord's
June
6 beat Worcestershire by 38 runs at Worcester
13 lost to Somerset by two wickets at Bath
20 lost to Northants by 22 runs at Northampton
27 beat Glamorgan by ten wickets at Lord's
July
4 beat Surrey by four wickets at Lord's
18 lost to Leicestershire by three wickets at Leicester
25 lost to Lancashire by five wickets at Lord's
August
1 lost to Warwickshire by seven wickets at Edgbaston
8 beat Derbyshire by seven wickets at Lord's
22 lost to Essex by 12 runs at Lord's
29 lost to Yorkshire by ten wickets at Bradford

John Player League Record

P	W	L	T	NR	Pts	Pos
16	7	9	0	0	28	13th

Benson and Hedges Cup
Group C

May
1 lost to Northants by seven wickets at Lord's
8 lost to Nottinghamshire by five wickets at Newark
15 beat Minor Counties (East) by 62 runs at Lord's
22 lost to Essex by seven wickets at Chelmsford

1977
Season Superb

With two cup final appearances in 1975 and a Championship win in 1976, Mike Brearley's Middlesex were now confirmed as one of the strongest and most efficient county sides of the day. In 1977 they were again at the forefront of honours, finishing top of the Championship once more, albeit sharing the title with Kent, and winning the Gillette Cup. In addition they reached the quarter-finals of the Benson and Hedges Cup with four straight wins in the group qualifying matches, and finished third in the John Player League. Add to that, individual successes at Test level, and some unique incidents in the club's — and, indeed, cricket's — history, and you have the ingredients for one of the most successful and interesting seasons which Middlesex ever enjoyed.

The Championship run took a different character to the outright success of the previous summer. Whereas the challengers had faded away in 1976, Kent and Gloucestershire maintained their assault right up to the final days and it was a unique decision to postpone a Championship match at Lord's and play it at Chelmsford a few days later which gave Middlesex that little bit of good fortune which every side needs to convert skill and enterprise into something more substantial. During the first two weeks in August, Middlesex had a disasterous time, losing to Leicestershire, Warwickshire and Northamptonshire, defeats surrounding a win over Surrey at Lord's.

Fixture problems usually work against clubs interested in honours, but on this occasion things worked out beautifully for Middlesex. Their Gillette Cup semi-final against Somerset could not be started on any of the original three days set aside to complete the game, and so the Schweppes County Championship between the two sides was postponed to fit

> **Middlesex's re-arranged Championship game against Somerset at Chelmsford in the penultimate match of 1977 was the first time they had played a home game away from Lord's since their match with Hampshire at Hornsey in 1959, and their first 'home' game outside Middlesex since the match at The Oval in 1939.**

Radley makes a big hit off Glamorgan's Richards at Lord's

in the knock-out game (this was the first season, incidentally, that the Championship had been sponsored). The new dates still found Lord's awash and it was only on what would have been the third day of the Championship match that play could start in the Gillette game. Middlesex, thus could have taken scant reward from the three-day game. But when it was played at Chelmsford five days later, they managed seven points which were vital to their cause.

Earlier in the season Middlesex felt they had been 'robbed' of an over during the run-chase against Gloucestershire at Lord's. It was a remarkable match with Brearley batting all day for his 145 before declaring at 343 for six. Gloucestershire then went from 48 without loss to 80 all out (Edmonds six for 18, Emburey four for 12) and then followed-on and amassed 337 (Edmonds took eight wickets, this time for 132). This left Middlesex to score 75 in twelve overs, according to umpires Bill Alley and Jack van Geloven. Brearley reasoned that the new regulations required every three minutes of an innings starting within the last hour should yield one over — thus Middlesex were entitled to thirteen, since there were thirty-eight minutes remaining. But Middlesex did not get their extra over and at the close they had stormed to 63 for seven. Against Surrey in August, Brearley's enterprise saw Middlesex take twenty wickets by the last day, without scoring a run in the match! They bowled Surrey out for 49, declared after one ball, bowled Surrey out again for 89 and knocked off the combined Surrey total for the loss of one wicket, a unique event.

The Gillette Cup run started with a thrilling two-wicket win in the last over of the match at Canterbury and it was a great pity that the semi-final against Somerset had to be reduced to a fifteen-over slog after the tie had fallen foul of the weather. Somerset were all out for 59 with two balls to spare and Middlesex got the runs for the loss of four wickets in less than twelve overs. In the final against Glamorgan, the Welshmen struggled to get the ball away on a wet outfield, Lord's only just being fit to play after more heavy rain. They totalled 177 for nine off their sixty overs with the left-handed Mike Llewellyn scoring a brave 62. His first three strokes were 4, 6, 4, off Gatting and one hit off Emburey carried nearly to the top tier of the pavilion. Glamorgan's hopes were high when Brearley went to the first ball of the Middlesex innings, but Radley steered them from possible disaster to a five-wicket win with an undefeated 85 which won him the Man of the Match Award.

Phil Edmonds took fourteen wickets in the controversial match with Gloucestershire at Lord's when Middlesex felt they had been 'robbed' of an over

Middlesex saw Fred Titmus retire before the start of the season, although the great all-rounder would be back for the occasional game in Middlesex colours. Jones suffered a bad back injury and played only seven games, but West Indian fast-bowler Wayne Daniel topped the averages with seventy-one wickets at 16.98. Selvey was bowling as well as ever and he took seventy-two, and spinners John Emburey (sixty-eight at 20.25), Edmonds (seventy-two at 24.11) and Featherstone (twenty-four at 29.37) completed the attack, sixty-six of Emburey's wickets coming in the last thirteen games. Radley, Gatting and Smith passed 1,000 runs, the averages being headed by Brearley who scored 820 runs at 68.33 when he was not leading England to victory in the Ashes series. He scored three centuries for Middlesex between Tests. Although Barlow disappointed in 1977, Gatting's form earned him a trip to Pakistan with MCC that winter, although his desire for quick runs meant that he had still not scored a first-class century.

FIRST CLASS RESULTS 1977
Championship Record

P	W	L	D	Pos
22	9	5	8	1st=

April
20-1 drew with MCC at Lord's
27-9 drew with Oxford University at The Parks

May
4-6 drew with Surrey at The Oval
11-13 drew with Kent at Lord's
18-20 beat Glamorgan by innings and 85 runs at Lord's
28-31 beat Nottinghamshire by 254 runs at Trent Bridge

June
1-3 lost to Kent by 238 runs at Dartford
4-7 beat Sussex by seven wickets at Lord's
11-14 drew with Hampshire at Portsmouth
15-17 beat Cambridge University by 83 runs at Fenners
18-20 lost to Derbyshire by innings and 177 runs at Ilkeston
25-8 beat Worcestershire by innings and 10 runs at Lord's

July
2-5 beat Nottinghamshire by 123 runs at Lord's
6-8 drew with Yorkshire at Lord's
9-12 drew with Essex at Southend
20-2 drew with Gloucestershire at Lord's
23-6 beat Essex by six wickets at Lord's
27-9 beat Yorkshire by 157 runs at Sheffield
July 30, **August** 1-2 lost to Leicestershire by 61 runs at Leicester

August
6-9 beat Surrey by nine wickets at Lord's
10-12 lost to Warwickshire by 34 runs at Lord's
13-16 lost to Northamptonshire by 128 runs at Wellingborough
20-2 drew with the Australians at Lord's
27-30 drew with Sussex at Hove
August 31, **September** 1-2 drew with Somerset at Chelmsford

September
7-9 beat Lancashire by 91 runs at Blackpool

Gillette Cup

June
29-30 beat Kent by two wickets in first round at Canterbury

July
13-14 beat Warwickshire by 31 runs in second round at Lord's

August
3 beat Hampshire by seven wickets in third round at Lord's

26 beat Somerset by six wickets in semi-final at Lord's

September
3 beat Glamorgan by five wickets in the final at Lord's

John Player League

May
1 lost to Nottinghamshire by six wickets at Trent Bridge
15 beat Lancashire by 1 run at Old Trafford
22 beat Warwickshire by 11 runs at Lord's
29 beat Somerset by 62 runs at Lord's

June
5 lost to Hampshire by 60 runs at Lord's
12 match with Gloucestershire abandoned at Gloucester
26 beat Worcestershire by eight wickets at Lord's

July
3 beat Leicestershire by 9 runs at Lord's
10 lost to Essex by 1 run at Southend
17 lost to Surrey by three wickets at The Oval
24 beat Northants by 14 runs at Lord's
31 beat Derbyshire by 16 runs at Derby

August
7 match with Yorkshire abandoned at Lord's
14 lost to Glamorgan by 35 runs at Cardiff
28 beat Sussex by five wickets at Lord's

September
4 beat Kent by five wickets at Maidstone

John Player League Record

P	W	L	NR	Pts	Pos
16	9	5	2	40	3rd

Benson and Hedges Cup
Group 'D'

April
23-4 beat Yorkshire by 12 runs at Lord's
30 beat Minor Counties (East) by six wickets at Lakenham

May
7-10 beat Essex by having lost fewer wickets at Lord's
21 beat Northants by 79 runs at Northampton

June
8 lost to Gloucestershire by 18 runs in quarter-final at Bristol

1978
England Expects

After winning the Championship in 1976 and sharing it in 1977 Middlesex slipped to third place in 1978, despite the fact that they won two more matches — and gained a further twenty-eight points — than the previous season. But it was the first part of the summer which undermined any real hopes that Middlesex would be back at the top with an outright win. The wickets at Lord's were never conducive to batting, thanks to the fact that a wet spring and equally poor summer was coupled with

Middlesex qualified for the Benson and Hedges Cup quarter-finals in 1978 by finishing second in their group:					
	P	W	L	NR	Pts
Sussex	4	3	1	0	9
Middlesex	4	3	1	0	9
Leicestershire	4	3	1	0	9
Northants	4	1	3	0	3
Minor Counties East	4	0	4	0	0

all Middlesex's home games being played by 15 August, which gave the ground staff a hopeless job.

Test calls, too, took their toll on Middlesex. Mike Brearley, Phil Edmonds and Clive Radley played in all six Tests against the New Zealanders and the Pakistanis, and John Emburey was called up for the last Test against New Zealand at Lord's. Middlesex simply did not have the reserves to draft in and the loss of three key players for much of the season was too great to overcome, particularly in a summer when Kent and Essex were in such fine form. Yet Middlesex's own form in the latter half of the season was certainly Championship material. Of their last ten games they won no less than eight but an equally fine spurt by Kent finally gave them the title, thirty-seven points ahead of Middlesex.

Individual performances varied and

Mike Selvey was the real workhorse of the Middlesex attack in 1978 when he became the last Middlesex bowler to take 100 wickets in a season

perhaps the form of Mike Brearley gave most cause for concern. Although he played in only two fewer games than in 1977, Brearley scored 500 fewer runs — his 1978 Middlesex aggregate was a meagre 320 — and in fact he played in one more innings this season. His average went down from 68.33 to just 26.66. Mike Smith was another batsman who had little joy in this dreadful summer, particularly in matches at Lord's. For the first time since 1969 he failed to hit 1,000 runs and, in fact, managed to get past 50 only three times with a top score of 63.

Clive Radley topped the averages with 41.46 and 539 runs in the nine games in which he played, and of the regular batsmen who, untroubled by the calls of the England selectors, played throughout the summer, Graham Barlow (985 runs at 33.96) and Mike Gatting (939 at 33.53) were the most successful, while Barbadian Roland Butcher, and Rhodesian Norman Featherstone, also weighed in with useful runs. When Middlesex beat Gloucester by an innings at Bristol, Butcher scored a brilliant 142 (two 6s and twenty-five 4s) and he and Featherstone (78) put on 154 for the fifth wicket after Middlesex had slumped to 75 for four. Mike Gatting reached his maiden first-class century against Yorkshire at Lord's and in the last home game of the season he hit Derbyshire for 128 as Middlesex again won by an innings.

Young wicketkeeper Ian Gould also chipped in with valuable runs, recovering from a nasty blow on the head when he misread a Colin Croft bouncer in early May on a lively Lord's track. Middlesex were chasing 169 to win. Gould had the double ignomony of being out hit-wicket and of being taken into hospital. Emburey collected the winning run with nine men out and Gould came back with 128 at Worcester later that season.

Wayne Daniel headed the bowling with seventy-five wickets at 14.50 each, but Mike Selvey was the real workhorse of the side. Selvey bowled 704.5 overs (compared to Daniel's 446.3) and captured ninety-four wickets at 19.31. Gatting, Edmonds, Emburey, Jones and Featherstone all gave valuable support and, although Jones was hampered by a back injury which perhaps dulled his edge, it was a tribute to his dedication that he came back at all after such a serious injury. Selvey, incidentally, took forty of his wickets in the last five games and he became the first Middlesex player to take 100 in a season since Titmus in 1971. Selvey's final haul in all games was 101 at 19.09.

Middlesex's one-day season is perhaps best left to lie in the statistics which tell their own story. After qualifying for the Benson and Hedges quarter-finals with three wins in four group games, Middlesex lost at Derby. The following month they were back at the County Ground to extract some revenge with a Gillette Cup win, but their joy was short-lived and Lancashire beat them in the next round. In the John Player League, only Warwickshire and Gloucestershire finished below Middlesex.

Off-spinner John Emburey was called up for the last Test against New Zealand

FIRST CLASS RESULTS 1978
Championship Record

P	W	L	D	No Dcsn	Pos
22	11	5	5	1	3rd

April
19-21 drew with MCC at Lord's
26-8 drew with Cambridge University at Fenners

May
3-5 match with Hampshire abandoned at Lord's
10-12 lost to Essex by 109 runs at Chelmsford
24-6 beat Lancashire by one wicket at Lord's
27-30 drew with Sussex at Lord's
May 31, June 1 beat Northants by ten wickets at Lord's

June
3-6 lost to Kent by six wickets at Lord's
10-13 lost to Warwickshire by six wickets at Edgbaston
14-16 drew with Yorkshire at Bradford
17-20 lost to Kent by 39 runs at Canterbury
24-7 beat Nottinghamshire by innings and 106 runs at Lord's

July
1-4 drew with Worcestershire at Worcester
5-7 drew with Essex at Lord's
8-11 lost to the New Zealanders by innings and 10 runs at Lord's
12-14 beat Leicestershire by one wicket at Lord's
15-18 beat Glamorgan by 176 runs at Swansea
26-8 beat Nottinghamshire by 111 runs at Trent Bridge

August
5-8 drew with Surrey at Lord's
9-11 beat Yorkshire by 167 runs at Lord's
12-15 beat Derbyshire by innings and 77 runs at Lord's
19-22 beat Somerset by eight wickets at Taunton
23-4 beat Gloucestershire by innings and 14 runs at Bristol
26-9 lost to Sussex by 107 runs at Hove

September
6-7 beat Surrey by ten wickets at The Oval

Gillette Cup

July
19-20 beat Derbyshire by 33 runs in second round at Derby

August
2-4 lost to Lancashire by 21 runs in third round at Old Trafford

John Player League

April
30 match with Northants abandoned at Lord's

May
7 beat Gloucestershire by seven wickets at Bristol
21 lost to Lancashire by six wickets at Lord's
28 lost to Leicestershire by 80 runs at Leicester

June
4 beat Kent by 39 runs at Lord's
11 beat Warwickshire by seven wickets at Edgbaston
25 beat Nottinghamshire by 51 runs at Lord's

July
2 lost to Worcestershire by 44 runs at Worcester
9 lost to Essex by nine wickets at Lord's
16 lost to Glamorgan by seven wickets at Swansea
30 lost to Yorkshire by four wickets at Lord's

August
6 match with Surrey abandoned at Lord's
13 beat Derbyshire by seven runs at Lord's
20 lost to Somerset by six wickets at Taunton
27 lost to Sussex by five wickets at Hove

September
3 lost to Hampshire by 26 runs at Bournemouth

John Player League Record

P	W	L	NR	Pts	Pos
16	5	9	2	24	15th

Benson and Hedges Cup
Group 'C' games

April
22 beat Minor Counties (East) by eight wickets at Ipswich
29 beat Northants by eight wickets at Lord's

May
13 beat Sussex by eight wickets at Hove
20 lost to Leicestershire by 10 runs at Lord's

June
7-8 lost to Derbyshire by 29 runs in quarter-final at Derby

1979

Temporary Setback

Middlesex slumped to sharing thirteenth spot in the Championship with Lancashire and for part of the season it looked likely that the county would even end up bottom of the table, a remarkable turnaround after the successes of the previous three summers. Indeed, by the middle of July, Middlesex were last. Only three victories in five games towards the end of that month and into August saved their faces. After that Middlesex were not successful again in the Championship and collected a miserly twenty-one points from their last five games. The reasons for this dramatic decline may be rested at the door of the England selectors — who took Brearley, Edmonds, and to a lesser degree, Gatting away from the club for long spells during the season. Or one can argue that the dreadful summer robbed Middlesex of points. Two matches at Lord's were abandoned without a ball being bowled and the first two matches of the season, at the end of a soggy spring, did not make the second innings. Even so, Middlesex were not alone in losing out to the weather and one cannot lay all the blame there.

Middlesex's three wins came against Leicestershire — a thrilling finish there — Essex and Glamorgan, both the latter sides being trounced handsomely as Middlesex found some of the form which had sent them to the top of English cricket not long before. The game at Leicester was remarkable for the transformation which Middlesex underwent after being bowled out for 97 in their first innings, when only Brearley, with 42, looked happy against the Leicestershire seam attack which had the visitors back in the pavilion before lunch.

Leicestershire's reply was far more accomplished and they reached 303 all out with David Gower falling to Embury just two short of what would have been a fine century. With a lead of 206 Leicestershire could feel confident that a win was their's for the taking, especially considering Middlesex's inept batting display the first time around. Middlesex certainly began in similar vein. Taylor had taken the last two Middlesex first innings wickets in successive balls and with his first ball in the second innings he had Smith caught by Tolchard to complete a fairly unusual hat-trick. But Roland Butcher came good with a century in only ninety-two minutes and, together with Radley, he helped to put on 162 for the fourth wicket. Middlesex reached 317, with Radley's contribution a priceless 81, which was a fair score, but which still left Leicestershire only 112 for victory. How-

Barbadian Roland Butcher scored a brilliant 142 at Bristol

ever, Wayne Daniel was bowling with fire in his belly and he removed the first three Leicestershire batsmen by the time the innings had reached 27 runs. Seven wickets were down for only 50 but Leicestershire still looked set when Tolchard set about grafting his side home. Wickets still fell, however, and with just three runs needed for a Leicestershire victory, Emburey induced Tolchard to play on and the innings was over at 109.

Middlesex's other two victories came in less breathtaking fashion — a ten-wicket win at Colchester and an innings defeat of Glamorgan at Lord's where Phil Edmonds scored a remarkable 141, reaching his century with a massive 6 into the Lord's pavilion. It was that innings, together with several other undefeated knocks, which helped Edmonds to top the Middlesex batting averages in 1979 with 56.85

> Middlesex became the first side to beat Essex in the 1979 Championship when they won at Colchester. Scores: Essex 106 (Daniel six for 38) and 225 (Fletcher 57, Pont 59); Middlesex 299 (Radley 55, Selvey 45, Fletcher five for 41) and 36 for no wicket.

from 398 runs. Barlow, Radley and Smith all topped 1,000 runs and it was good to see Mike Smith back to something like his old form. Smith started the season with an unbeaten 100 in his first innings, against Warwickshire at Lord's, and he made four more in the Championship before the season was through. Brearley's absence with England obviously brought his county aggregate down again and he finished fourth in the averages with 37.72 from 416

Somerset jubilation, Middlesex sorrow. Mike Brearley walks dejectedly away after being caught by Taylor off Garner for 2 runs in the Gillette Cup semi-final at Lord's

runs which included an undefeated 148 against Gloucestershire at Lord's.

Wayne Daniel took fifty-two wickets at 22.50 each to head the averages and Featherstone came second with twenty-three at 24.69, although sadly, the Rhodesian was not retained by Middlesex at the season's end. Emburey and Selvey both topped fifty wickets and Edmonds took thirty-two in his ten Championship matches. Gatting hardly bowled at all and his main role was that of batsman when he scored 557 runs at an average of 32.76. In all, Middlesex's bowling never looked penetrative enough and the side's bowling bonus points tally was fifteen short of the previous summer's total. In the one-day games Middlesex cricket looked infinitely healthier, though they failed here, too, to win any honours.

FIRST CLASS RESULTS 1979
Championship Record

	P	W	L	D	No Dcsn	Pos
	22	3	3	14	2	13th =

May
2-4   drew with Warwickshire at Lord's
9-11   drew with Essex at Lord's
16-18   drew with Kent at Lord's
26-9   match with Sussex abandoned at Lord's

June
2-5   drew with Gloucestershire at Lord's
9-12   drew with Derbyshire at Derby
13-15   match with Nottinghamshire abandoned at Lord's
16-19   drew with Surrey at Lord's
20-2   drew with Kent at Tunbridge Wells
23-6   lost to Lancashire by six wickets at Old Trafford

July
7-10   drew with Surrey at The Oval
11-13   drew with Yorkshire at Lord's
25-7   beat Leicestershire by 2 runs at Leicester
28-31   lost to Yorkshire by six wickets at Scarborough

August
1-3   beat Essex by ten wickets at Colchester
4-7   drew with Northants at Northampton
11-14   beat Glamorgan by innings and 34 runs at Lord's
15-17   drew with Hampshire at Portsmouth
18-21   drew with Somerset at Lord's
25-8   drew with Sussex at Hove
29-31   lost to Worcestershire by 165 runs at Lord's

September
5-7   drew with Nottinghamshire at Trent Bridge

Gillette Cup

July
18   beat Hampshire by two wickets in second round at Lord's

August
8-9   beat Yorkshire by 70 runs in third round at Lord's
22   lost to Somerset by seven wickets in semi-final at Lord's

John Player League

April
29   match with Nottinghamshire abandoned at Trent Bridge

May
6   beat Hampshire by 12 runs at Lord's
20   match with Leicestershire abandoned at Lord's
27   lost to Northants on faster scoring rate at Milton Keynes

June
3   beat Gloucestershire by four wickets at Lord's
10   beat Derbyshire by six wickets at Chesterfield
17   lost to Worcestershire by 5 runs at Lord's
24   beat Lancashire by 81 runs at Old Trafford

July
1   beat Warwickshire by 82 runs at Lord's
8   lost to Surrey by 12 runs at The Oval
28   beat Yorkshire by 43 runs at Scarborough

August
12   beat Glamorgan by 68 runs at Lord's
19   lost to Somerset by 28 runs at Lord's
26   lost to Essex by 99 runs at Chelmsford

September
2   beat Sussex by five wickets at Lord's
9   beat Kent by 55 runs at Canterbury

John Player League Record

	P	W	L	NR	Pts	Pos
	16	9	5	2	40	4th =

Benson and Hedges Cup
Group 'D'

April 28-30, May 1   beat Nottinghamshire on faster scoring rate at Trent Bridge

May
5   beat Minor Counties (North) by six wickets at Lord's
12   beat Kent by 105 runs at Canterbury
23-5   no result in match with Yorkshire at Lord's

June
6   lost to Yorkshire by four wickets in quarter final at Lord's

1980

Team of the Decade?

After their poor Championship record of the previous summer Middlesex came back to win the title in 1980 and in doing so they also took the Gillette Cup, reached the semi-final of the Benson and Hedges Cup and finished third in the John Player League. Not since four trophies became on offer had one team scooped so much success. The nearest had been Middlesex themselves in 1977. Of course, Middlesex had threatened to do well in the one-day cups and league in 1979 and they carried that momentum through to become the best exponents of 'instant' cricket in England; and they proved that their indifferent Championship, coming after three years of triumph, was merely a flash in the pan. Mike Brearley had moulded together a team as expert and professional as any cricket has seen in terms of combining victory in the three-day and one-day game.

Probably the most significant factor behind this success was the recruitment of the giant South African fast bowler, Vincent van der Bijl, who was signed for this season only, when it was assumed that the West Indian tourists would take Wayne Daniel. When the West Indians decided they could manage without the Barbadian paceman, Middlesex found themselves embarrassed by the luxury of having undoubtedly the most hostile opening attack in the country. The South African pounded the ball in from a tremendous height (he was also adept at hitting a few 6s which did not come amiss in one-day cricket), while Daniel was again the sort of bowler who brought the ball through at chest height to county circuit batsmen.

In addition to van der Bijl, Middlesex had the use of another paceman, Simon Hughes, and the youngster, while not making the profound contribution of the South African, gave Middlesex great hopes for his future prospects. Van der Bijl finished top of the bowling averages with eighty-five wickets at 14.72, figures which put him second in the national averages and only marginally behind Richard Hadlee (who had fifty-six fewer wickets, incidentally). Merry played in four games but with fourteen wickets at 15.57 came second in the Middlesex averages, to be followed by Hughes (eighteen at 19.55), Emburey (sixty-one at 19.70), Daniel (sixty-seven at 21.70), Titmus (twelve at 26.08) and Edmonds (thirty-four at 27.35). Fred Titmus played in five games and, after starting his career in 1949, had the distinction of appearing for Middlesex in five different decades. Mike Selvey, denied the new ball by Daniel and Van der Bijl, took twenty-six wickets at 38.96 each. Edmonds, with a knee injury, and Emburey, through Test calls, missed several Championship games.

Radley and Brearley topped 1,000 runs, the Middlesex captain now playing a full season after stepping down as England skipper. Radley headed the averages with 52.00, Gatting came second with 602 runs and 50.16, and Brearley third with 47.48. Kent wicketkeeper Paul Downton moved to Lord's, with the return of Alan Knott to county cricket, and the youngster gave Brearley a bonus by blossoming out as an opening batsman, although his arrival meant that Ian Gould, his predecessor behind the stumps, left the club to seek fame elsewhere. Wilf Slack, Roland Butcher and Mike Smith all failed as openers and Smith played in only four games.

Butcher's story was different. He fought his way back, scored 153 not out against Hampshire at Lord's, followed up that with 179 at Scarborough, and was selected for England in the Prudential Cup games and for the winter tour to his native Caribbean. Gatting's appearances were curtailed by Test calls, but Graham Barlow enjoyed a good season with the bat, scoring 952 runs at 43.27. In this Middlesex Championship win there were no last-minute thrills. Middlesex went to the top on 3 June, after beating Somerset at Taunton, and after that they always looked certain winners.

The John Player League season started off with six straight wins and ended with

---

Mike Brearley guided Middlesex to an easy Gillette Cup final win over Surrey at Lord's. Surrey were all out for 201 in their sixty overs with the wickets being shared around. Middlesex reached their target with seven wickets and six overs to spare. Brearley made an undefeated 96 to take the Man of the Match Award, judged by Ian Botham, and Roland Butcher weighed in with an exciting undefeated 50 which included two 6s off Knight and one off Jackman.

---

four more; but in between, Middlesex suffered a lean patch, including one game abandoned, and that was enough to deny them what would have been a staggering

treble. They finished just four points behind the winners, Warwickshire. The quarter-final match in the Benson and Hedges Cup was a bizarre affair with Imran Khan opening with eight wides in his first five overs and then being involved in an incident with Brearley as Middlesex neared victory. Imran complained to umpire Jack van Geloven about short-pitched deliveries from Daniel. Wessel's hand had earlier been broken and when Pigot was hit, the Sussex player decided to object. Brearley came up to express a view and to the astonishment of the Lord's crowd it appeared for a few seconds as if the two men would come to blows. The TCCB left it to the counties to sort out and Imran was later reprimanded by Sussex, while Middlesex expressed their regret at the captain's involvement. Middlesex were just eleven runs short of reaching the final when they met Northants. Only Gatting (91) and Slack (42) looked likely to take them through against the fine bowling from Sarfraz.

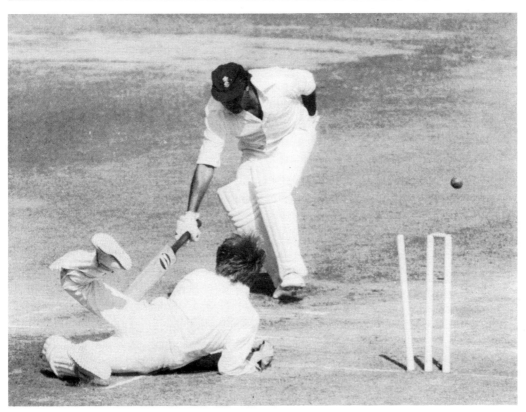

Gillette Cup Final at Lord's and Surrey's Pocock narrowly misses being stumped

Mike Brearley holds the Gillette Cup, the last time the competition will be held

FIRST CLASS RESULTS 1980
Championship Record

P	W	L	D	Pos
22	10	2	10	1st

April 30, **May** 1-2 drew with Nottinghamshire at Trent Bridge

May
- 3-6   drew with Lancashire at Lord's
- 7-9   drew with Cambridge University at Fenners
- 24-7   beat Sussex by innings and 5 runs at Lord's
- 28-30   drew with Worcestershire at Worcester

May 31, **June** 2-3 beat Somerset by seven wickets at Taunton

June
- 4-6   beat Surrey by innings and 58 runs at Lord's
- 7-10   drew with Yorkshire at Lord's
- 14-17   drew with Surrey at The Oval
- 18-20   beat Essex by eight wickets at Southend
- 21-4   drew with Oxford University at The Parks

June 28-30, **July** 1 drew with Warwickshire at Edgbaston

July
- 5-8   drew with Northants at Lord's
- 9-11   beat Hampshire by five wickets at Lord's
- 23-5   beat Yorkshire by eight wickets at Scarborough
- 26-9   drew with Kent at Lord's

August
- 2-5   beat Essex by innings and 4 runs at Lord's
- 6-7   lost to Leicestershire by innings and 100 runs at Lord's
- 9-12   lost to Gloucestershire by six wickets at Cheltenham
- 16-19   beat Nottinghamshire by innings and 17 runs at Lord's
- 20-2   beat Derbyshire by nine wickets at Uxbridge
- 23-6   drew with Sussex at Hove

August 30, **September** 1-2 beat Glamorgan by 72 runs at Cardiff

September
- 3-5   drew with Kent at Canterbury

Gillette Cup

July
- 2   beat Ireland by five wickets in first round at Lord's
- 16   beat Nottinghamshire by four wickets in second round at Trent Bridge
- 30   beat Worcestershire by ten wickets in third round at Worcester

August
- 13-14   beat Sussex by 64 runs in the semi-final at Hove

September
- 6   beat Surrey by seven wickets in the final at Lord's

John Player League

May
- 4   beat Lancashire by 7 runs at Lord's
- 18   beat Worcestershire by nine wickets at Worcester
- 25   beat Northants by seven wickets at Lord's

June
1 beat Somerset by 122 runs at Taunton
8 beat Yorkshire by three wickets at Lord's
15 beat Surrey by ten wickets at Lord's
29 lost to Warwickshire by five wickets at Edgbaston

July
6 lost to Derbyshire by eight wickets at Lord's
20 match with Leicestershire abandoned at Leicester
27 lost to Kent by 13 runs at Lord's

August
3 lost to Essex by 57 runs at Lord's
10 lost to Gloucestershire by 55 runs at Cheltenham
17 beat Nottinghamshire on faster scoring rate at Lord's
24 beat Sussex by 21 runs at Hove
31 beat Glamorgan by 11 runs at Cardiff

September
7 beat Hampshire by five wickets at Bournemouth

P	W	L	NR	Pts	Pos
16	10	5	1	42	3rd

Benson and Hedges Cup Group 'D'

May
10 beat Surrey by eight wickets at Lord's
14 beat Hampshire by seven wickets at Southampton
17 beat Somerset by 1 run at Taunton
22 beat Kent by 80 runs at Lord's

June
11 beat Sussex by 29 runs in quarter-final at Lord's
25-6 lost to Northants by 11 runs in semi-final at Lord's

1981

The Run Makers

Although Middlesex failed to hold on to the Championship — the title went to Trent Bridge for the first time since 1929 — the 1981 season brought plenty of interest for the club's supporters. Middlesex were always around the top of the table, though when Notts finally took control there was never any doubt about the eventual outcome of the Championship, and several landmarks were reached during the county's season. There was controversy when the two sides met at Trent Bridge in late June. Hughes took a career-best six for 102 in Notts' first innings and Paul Downton, dropped by England, held six catches in the same innings. But the real drama came when the umpires allowed Middlesex an extra five minutes bowling in the Notts' second

innings after an injury to Eddie Hemmings. Middlesex bowled out their opponents to win by 112 runs, and Notts were left to query the decision with the TCCB. In the previous match, against Essex at Ilford, Middlesex fielded an unregistered wicketkeeper, Chilton Taylor, and were fined £300 and lost seven bonus points.

Middlesex had searched hard for an overseas player during the close season and their first target was India's Kapil Dev. But Kapil had complications with a contract signed with Lancashire League Nelson, and Middlesex turned their attention to Australia's Jeff Thomson. It was a controversial move and ironically Thomson played only eight games before returning to Brisbane after a hernia oper-

The opening Schweppes Championship match of the season and Brearley hooks John Lever of Essex at Lord's

ation. Thomson claimed twenty-three wickets at 22.69 runs each by the time he was forced out of the side, and his pace partner, Wayne Daniel, helped himself to sixty-seven wickets at 22.29 each. Against Lancashire at Southport, Daniel did the hat-trick for the first time in his career. But it was the spinners who triumphed in 1981. John Emburey topped the averages with fifty-nine victims (average 21.28) and Phil Edmonds took most wickets with seventy-three (average 24.84). Edmonds took his first hat-trick at Leicester on 3 September. Monteith, Hughes, Merry and Selvey all weighed in with useful wickets, Merry playing in just seven games.

The Middlesex batsmen began to re-write some of the county's records. Against Kent at Lord's on 17 July, Graham Barlow (174 not out) and Wilf Slack (181 not out) created a new first-wicket record for the club with an unbroken stand of 367, beating the 312 set by Eric Russell and Mike Harris against Pakistan in 1967. Both batsmen passed their previous bests and in the next game, against Worcestershire at Lord's, Slack scored 248 not out. But

> Mike Selvey's 57 against Essex at Ilford was his first half-century after thirteen years in the first-class game. Nine days later he scored a second half-century. Middlesex took the Holt Products Trophy and £3,500 for the best performance by a county against the 1981 Australians.

Slack, despite hitting the season's highest score, was dropped for the following match, against Lancashire in the Nat West Trophy, to make way for Brearley, who returned from leading England to their amazing Test win at Headingley. Middlesex were still piling on the runs at the season's end when Gatting (186 not out) and Brearley (145) added 338 for the third wicket at Derby. Gatting headed the Middlesex averages with 1,026 runs at 68.40, and Brearley, Slack, Barlow and Radley all passed the 1,000-runs mark. Seventeen-year-old Colin Metson made his first-class debut behind the stumps at Derby.

The final match of the season at Derby. Brearley puts New Zealand Test opener John Wright under pressure. Middlesex wicketkeeper is seventeen-year old Colin Metson making his first-class debut

> **Against Surrey at Uxbridge, when Middlesex won by six wickets, the crowd were treated to some vintage cricket with 1,113 runs scored in two and a half days, and plenty of spin bowling in gloriously sunny conditions. Scores: Surrey 411 (Clinton 114) and 145 (Emburey five for 37), Middlesex 392 for eight declared (Gatting 169) and 165 for four.**

Middlesex failed to retain the Championship, but there was every indication that they would be back to put in a strong challenge in 1982. In their one-day competitions, the Benson and Hedges Cup fell foul of the weather, only one group game being completed. And in the new Nat West Trophy, they fell at the first hurdle. The John Player League, too, was a disappointment. Three games were ruined by rain, the last seven were lost, and Middlesex finished in fifteenth place. Cricket has come a long way since the days of Southgate's Walker brothers — but for Middlesex, success is still the hallmark. It is perhaps ironic that Mike Brearley, who in an earlier age would have been the very epitome of the cavalier amateur batsman from university, should be one of the most astute, dedicated and professional captains that Middlesex, and indeed cricket in general, has ever seen.

FIRST CLASS RESULTS 1981
Championship Record

P	W	L	D	No Dcsn	Pos
22	9	3	9	1	4th

April 29-30, **May** 1 drew with MCC at Lord's

May
- 6-8   drew with Essex at Lord's
- 13-15   beat Yorkshire by 81 runs at Headingley
- 23-6   match with Sussex abandoned at Lord's
- 27-9   drew with Nottinghamshire at Uxbridge

June
- 3-5   drew with Hampshire at Basingstoke
- 6-9   drew with Somerset at Lord's
- 13-15   drew with Australians at Lord's
- 17-19   lost to Essex by 95 runs at Ilford
- 27-30   beat Nottinghamshire by 112 runs at Trent Bridge

July
- 1-3   beat Kent by one wicket at Maidstone
- 15-17   drew with Kent at Lord's
- 18-21   drew with Worcestershire at Lord's
- 29-31   beat Lancashire by eight wickets at Southport

August
- 1-4   drew with Gloucestershire at Lord's
- 8-11   beat Warwickshire by 118 runs at Lord's
- 12-14   drew with Northants at Northampton
- 15-17   lost to Surrey by ten wickets at The Oval
- 22-5   beat Glamorgan by innings and 36 runs at Lord's
- 26-8   beat Yorkshire by six wickets at Lord's

August 29-31, **September** 1 lost to Sussex by ten wickets at Hove

September
- 2-4   beat Leicestershire by innings and 62 runs at Leicester
- 9-11   beat Surrey by six wickets at Uxbridge
- 12-15   drew with Derbyshire at Derby

Nat West Trophy

July
- 22-4   lost to Lancashire by 42 runs in second round at Old Trafford

John Player League

May
- 10   match with Hampshire abandoned at Lord's
- 17   beat Surrey by five wickets at The Oval
- 24   match with Sussex abandoned at Lord's
- 31   match with Yorkshire abandoned at Bradford

June
- 7   lost to Somerset on scoring rate at Lord's
- 21   beat Leicestershire by five wickets at Lord's
- 28   beat Nottinghamshire by 34 runs at Trent Bridge

July

12   lost to Lancashire by three wickets at Old Trafford

19   beat Worcestershire by six wickets at Lord's

26   lost to Northants by 4 runs at Lord's

August

2   lost to Gloucestershire by eight wickets at Lord's

9   lost to Warwickshire on scoring rate at Lord's

23   lost to Glamorgan by 37 runs at Lord's

30   lost to Kent by five wickets at Canterbury

September

6   lost to Essex by three wickets at Chelmsford

13   lost to Derbyshire on scoring rate at Derby

John Player League Record

P	W	L	NR	Pts	Pos
16	4	9	3	22	15th

Benson and Hedges Cup
Group 'D'

May

9   lost to Hampshire by one wicket at Lord's

16   match with Minor Counties abandoned at Slough

19   match with Sussex abandoned at Lord's

21   match with Surrey abandoned at The Oval

Middlesex Records

BATTING RECORDS

Record partnership for each wicket

1st	367*	G. Barlow and W. Slack v Kent at Lord's 1981
2nd	380	F. Tarrant and J. W. Hearne v Lancashire at Lord's 1914
3rd	424*	W. Edrich and D. Compton v Somerset at Lord's 1948
4th	325	J. W. Hearne and E. Hendren v Hampshire at Lord's 1919
5th	338	R. Lucas and T. O'Brien v Sussex at Hove 1895
6th	227	C. Radley and F. Titmus v South Africans at Lord's 1965
7th	271*	E. Hendren and F. T. Mann v Notts at Trent Bridge 1925
8th	182*	M. Doll and H. Murrell v Notts at Lord's 1913
9th	160*	E. Hendren and F. Durston v Essex at Leyton 1927
10th	230	R. Nicholls and W. Roche v Kent at Lord's 1899

* unbroken stand

BOWLING RECORDS

Ten wickets in an innings

G. O. Allen 10 for 40 v Lancashire at Lord's 1929

A. E. Trott 10 for 42 v Somerset at Taunton 1900

G. Burton 10 for 59 v Surrey at The Oval 1888

V. E. Walker 10 for 104 v Lancashire at Old Trafford 1865

Most wickets in a match

G. Burton 16 for 114 v Yorkshire at Sheffield 1888

J. T. Hearne 16 for 114 v Lancashire at Old Trafford 1898

F. Tarrant 16 for 176 v Lancashire at Old Trafford 1914

Highest innings by Middlesex
642 for 3 declared v Hampshire at Southampton 1923

Lowest innings by Middlesex
20 v MCC at Lord's 1864

Highest innings against Middlesex
665 by West Indians at Lord's 1939

Lowest innings against Middlesex
31 by Gloucestershire at Bristol 1924

Highest individual score for Middlesex
331 not out by J. Robertson v Worcestershire at Worcester 1949

Most centuries scored for Middlesex in career
119 by E. Hendren 1907-37

Most runs in a season
W. Edrich, 2,650 at 85.48 average, 1947

Most times 1,000 runs in a season
E. Hendren, 20

Most runs in career
E. Hendren, 40,302 at 48.82 average

Hat Tricks
There have been over 25 instances of Middlesex players taking a hat-trick for the county. Frank Tarrant achieved the feat four times for the county alone (including four wickets in four balls at Bristol in 1907). Albert Trott took two hat-tricks in the same innings against Somerset at Lord's in 1907, including four wickets in four balls in the first one.

Most wickets in a season
158 F. Titmus 1955

Most times 100 wickets in a season
F. Titmus, 11

Most wickets in career
F. Titmus, 2,358 at 21.26 each 1949-80

All-Rounders Double for Middlesex
F. Tarrant 6 times; J. W. Hearne 4 times; F. Titmus 4 times; N. Haig 1

FIELDING

Most catches in an innings
F. Tarrant, 6 v Essex at Leyton 1906

Most catches in a match
A. F. J. Ford, 7 v Gloucestershire at Lord's 1882.
F. Tarrant, 7 v Essex at Leyton 1906

Most catches in a season
P. Parfitt, 46 in 1960 and 46 in 1966

Most catches in a career
E. Hendren, 562, 1907-37

WICKETKEEPING

Most dismissals in an innings
W. Price, 7 (all caught) v Yorkshire at Lord's 1937

Most dismissals in a match
M. Turner, 9 (6ct, 3st) v Notts at Prince's 1875
J. Murray, 9 (8ct, 1st) v Hampshire at Lord's 1965

Most dismissals in a season
J. Murray, 99 (92ct, 7st) 1960

Most dismissals in career
J. Murray, 1,223 (1,024ct, 199st) 1952-75

All above records correct to 30 September 1981